Table of Contents

UNDERSTANDING THE INSURANCE INDUSTRY
2017 Edition

Published by A.M. Best

A.M. BEST COMPANY, INC.
Oldwick, NJ
CHAIRMAN & PRESIDENT **Arthur Snyder III**
EXECUTIVE VICE PRESIDENT **Karen B. Heine**
SENIOR VICE PRESIDENTS **Alessandra L. Czarnecki,
Thomas J. Plummer**

A.M. BEST RATING SERVICES, INC.
Oldwick, NJ
CHAIRMAN & PRESIDENT **Larry G. Mayewski**
EXECUTIVE VICE PRESIDENT **Matthew C. Mosher**
SENIOR MANAGING DIRECORS **Douglas A. Collett,
Edward H. Easop, Stefan W. Holzberger,
Andrea Keenan, James F. Snee**

ART & PRODUCTION
GROUP VICE PRESIDENT
PUBLICATION & NEWS SERVICES **Lee McDonald**
SENIOR MANAGER **Susan L. Browne**
DESIGN/GRAPHICS **Angel M. Negrón**

Tell Us What You Think
Is this publication helpful to you?
Did you find the information you were looking for?
What other information do you wish we had included?
Send your thoughts to *news@ambest.com*.

ISBN: 978-1979201353
ISSN:2375-7280

Visit *http://guides.ambest.com* to order additional copies.

For Those Interested in The Insurance Industry

A.M. Best Company publishes *Understanding the Insurance Industry* to provide a clear picture of how the insurance industry operates, generates revenue and provides opportunities for people of varied talents and interests.

It's designed to provide readers with a high-level overview of the insurance industry, particularly how it operates in the United States. It's also designed to be a gentle and broad introduction to the insurance industry for students, new employees, prospects and those who would like to learn more about one of the most interesting and important financial services industries.

We've designed this book in six sections: the property/casualty sector (also known as nonlife insurance), life, health, reinsurance and alternative risk transfer, and the function of A.M. Best in the industry.

Articles were prepared by members of A.M. Best's editorial team. Some content is extracted from *Special Reports* produced by A.M. Best, from articles in *Best's Review* magazine and from original reporting specifically for this edition.

Additional copies of this book are available by ordering online. Details are enclosed in the book. If you have suggestions for future topics or areas of focus, please send your comments to *news@ambest.com.*

Even more information, including monthly analytic broadcasts, topical webinars and other multiplatform resources are available at *www.ambest.com.*

Insurance: Financial Protection From Risks

Insurance protects against the financial risks that are present at all stages of people's lives and businesses. Insurers protect against loss — of a car, a house, even a life — and pay the policyholder or designee a benefit in the event of that loss. Those who suffer the loss present a claim and request payment under the insurance coverage terms, which are outlined in a policy. Insurers typically cannot replace the item lost but can provide financial compensation to address the economic hardship caused by a loss.

All aspects of life include exposure to risk. Individuals and businesses are presented with a choice: accept the consequences of a possible loss, or seek insurance coverage in the event of a loss, reducing their exposure to risk. Those who don't procure insurance coverage are responsible for the full loss. Those who obtain coverage succeed in "transferring the risk" to another organization, typically an insurance company.

Purchasing insurance is the most common risk transfer mechanism for the majority of people and organizations. The money paid from the insured is known as the premium. In return, the insurer agrees to pay a designated benefit in the event of the agreed-upon loss.

Insurance takes advantage of concepts known as risk pooling and the law of large numbers. Many policyholders pay a relatively small amount in premiums to protect themselves against a possible larger loss. When a sufficient number of insureds make that same choice, the funds available to pay claims increase and the chances of any single person or group exhausting the available funds grow smaller.

In risk pooling, insurers can accept a diverse and large number of risks, so long as many people participate in the insurance process, and they have an unequal likelihood of making a claim. Although an insurer may accept risks from a large number of people, only a small portion of those are likely to suffer an insured financial loss during the period of insurance coverage. Risk pooling allows insurers to pay claims to the few from the funds of the many.

What insurers sell is protection against economic loss. These losses are outlined in contracts or documents known as insurance policies. Insurers that cover life and health usually do not cover property or liability, which is the domain of property/casualty insurers.

Life and health insurers cover three general areas:

- Protection against premature death.
- Protection against poor health or unexpected medical costs.
- Protection against outliving one's financial resources.

Nonlife insurers, known as the property/casualty sector in the United States and Canada, in general offer two basic forms of coverage:

- Property insurance provides protection against most risks to tangible property occurring as the result of fire, flood, earthquake, theft or other perils.
- Casualty, or liability, insurance is broader than property and is often coverage of an individual or organization for negligent acts or omissions.

A well-known form of casualty insurance, auto liability coverage, protects drivers in the event they are found to be at fault in an accident.

A driver found to be at fault may be responsible for medical expenses, repairs and restitution to other people involved in the incident.

Insurance Density – Annual Per Capita Insurance Premiums (2016)

Source: Swiss Re *sigma* and Axco

is underwriting profit same as surplus?

How Insurers Make Money

Insurance companies primarily make money in two ways: from investments and by generating an underwriting profit—that is, collecting premium that exceeds insured losses and related expenses.

It all begins with underwriting. Insurers, whether life or nonlife, must assess the risk and gauge the likelihood of claims and the value of those claims.

The companies invest assets that are set aside to pay claims brought by policyholders. The interval between the time the insurer receives the premium and the time a claim against that policy is made is known as the float. *FLOAT.*

If an insurer has predominantly short-term obligations, asset portfolios should be relatively liquid in nature (i.e., publicly traded bonds, commercial paper and cash).

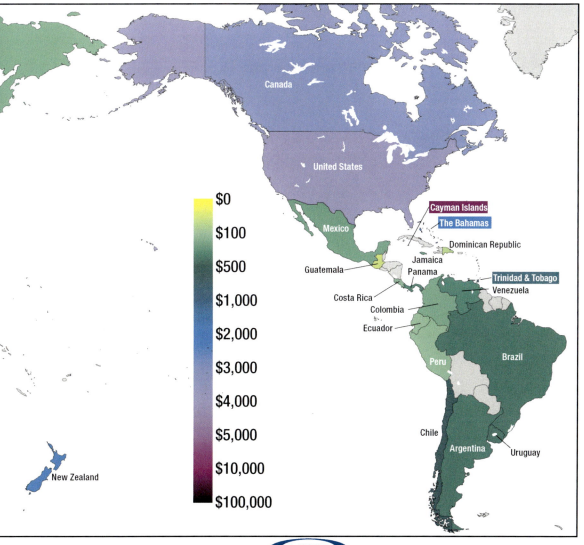

If the needs are long term, a portfolio containing fixed-income securities, such as bonds and mortgage loans, may also include preferred and common stocks, real estate and a variety of alternative asset classes.

Life insurers also establish separate accounts for nonguaranteed insurance products, such as variable life insurance or annuities, which provide for investment decisions by policyholders.

Property/casualty insurers traditionally have been more conservative with the asset side of their balance sheets, primarily due to the high levels of risk on the liability side. For example, catastrophe losses can wipe out years of accumulated premiums in some lines.

In the end, the insurer builds up a diversified portfolio of financial assets that will eventually be used to pay off any future claims brought by policyholders.

The global recession of the previous decade hurt nearly all aspects of the insurance industry, as many companies experienced declining revenues and investment losses. Those companies that were trading riskier instruments such as credit default swaps suffered most severely.

Few winners emerged; however, the mutual insurance sector managed to remain somewhat unscathed by the downturn. Meanwhile, a continuing low interest rate environment limits the ability of life and other insurers to benefit from fixed investments such as bonds.

The Economics of Insurance

U.S. Insurance Industry Jobs by Sector

Direct Life Insurance Carriers	351,700
Direct Health & Medical Insurance Carriers	476,400
Direct Property & Casualty Insurers	570,800
Direct Title Insurance and Other Direct Insurance Carriers	95,100
Reinsurance Carriers	25,500
Insurance Agencies and Brokerages	785,200
Claims Adjusting	57,200
Third-Party Administration of Insurance Funds	186,900

Source: U.S. Department of Labor

More than 2,600 single property/casualty companies and 770 single life/health insurance companies are included in A.M. Best's files for the United States and Canada. A.M. Best's global database includes statements on more than 11,000 insurance companies worldwide. Insurers pay claims in property, liability, life, health, annuity, reinsurance and other forms of coverage. In the United States alone, the broader insurance industry provides employment to 2.5 million people.

Insurance organizations play a vital role in the U.S. and other economies. They protect individuals and businesses from financial loss. The money they receive as premiums is invested in the economy. Protection from financial loss provides a sense of security to individuals and businesses, which are freer to pursue business and personal opportunities without worrying about financial devastation. Businesses can afford to purchase real estate and equipment, to hire more employees and fund travel and expansion.

Premiums collected from insureds, often known as policyholders, are invested by insurance organizations until they are paid out. Investor Warren Buffett has famously championed the value of "float"—funds held by insurance companies until they must be paid—as an important source of investment capital. However, insurers must be cautious and risk-averse with the majority of their investments, both to satisfy regulators' demands and to be able at any moment to pay claims.

Insurance companies are large holders of bonds, particularly those issued by corporations and similar sources. They invest small portions of their available funds in stocks. Life insurers have traditionally played larger roles in real estate investments, although a portion of those investments has shifted from direct ownership of commercial properties to more liquid investments in real estate investment trusts and the like. Insurers have also funded mortgages for commercial borrowers and developers, who in turn use the money to build commercial centers, shopping centers, apartments, warehouses and houses.

The insurance industry is part of the larger financial services industry, which includes banks, brokerages, mutual funds, credit unions, trust companies, pension funds and similar organizations. Traditional barriers between industries have disappeared in part. Mutual funds can be sold by insurance companies and banks. Equities brokers handle cash management accounts. Banks have become active sellers of life insurance and annuities and other insurance products. Insurers themselves have developed products that include savings, protection and investment elements.

How Insurance Is Sold

Insurance is sold through a variety of channels, including face-to-face by insurance agents and brokers, over the internet, through the mail, by phone, in workplace programs and through associations and affinity groups.

Insurance agents generally represent the insurance company. Insurance brokers usually represent the insured client but can sometimes act as an insurance agent.

The insurance agent (or producer) can be a key component in the underwriting process by taking the role of intermediary.

Top 10 Global Brokers by Total Revenue (2016)
(US$ billions)

Marsh & McLennan Cos.
Aon Plc.
Willis Towers Watson
Arthur J. Gallagher & Co.
BB&T Insurance Holdings Inc.
Brown & Brown Inc.
Hub International Ltd.
Jardine Lloyd Thompson Group plc
Lockton Inc.
USI Insurance Services

0   3   6   9   12   15

Source: *Best's Review* magazine

Unlike the underwriter, the agent is positioned to meet with the applicant, ask pertinent questions and gauge responses. Information gathered from the interview may become the basis the underwriter uses in decision-making. As a benefit to the consumer, many agents—called independent agents—represent several insurance companies, and may have a better view of each company's risk-selection threshold.

A "captive" or "tied" agent works primarily with a single insurer or a group of insurers, and may receive business leads or some sort of special preference for having that relationship. The insurer often offers benefits, such as health coverage, marketing support and training to the captive agent.

Generally speaking, insurance companies with a captive agent force also may see better policyholder retention. For starters, independent agents are less likely to follow policyholders from one state to another when they move; many independent agents are not licensed in multiple states. Larger insurance organizations may have the resources to track and follow an insured, and they may alert a new agent in the area to where the policyholder has moved.

In addition to agents, the following channels are used to get the business of insurance done:

Brokers: These producers do not necessarily work for an insurance company. Instead, the broker will place policies for clients with the carrier offering the most appropriate rate and coverage terms. The broker is rewarded by the carrier, often at a rate that differs than that paid to the carrier's agents.

Managing General Agents: These individuals or organizations are granted the authority by an insurer to perform a wide array of functions that can include placing business and issuing policies.

Agents are paid commissions based on the value and type of products they sell. Some insurers pay brokers additional compensation based on how the business performs.

Direct Sales: Direct selling of insurance to consumers through mail, internet or telephone solicitations has exploded in recent years. Insurance companies can bypass commissions by removing the agent from the transaction, although marketing and other associated costs can offset the savings.

Increasingly, online relationships are facilitated by traffic aggregators—basically an alternative term for price-comparison sites. The aggregator service links the consumer to the insurer. Aggregator companies receive a commission from product providers when a policy is sold. They also may charge a fee based on any click-through to those providers.

The aggregator service can present challenges on two fronts: The site encourages consumers to select insurance policies based almost exclusively on price, and direct sales are a threat to the independent agent.

Important Functions Of Insurance Organizations

Investment: Insurers look to investment managers to make sure they have the funds available to pay claims in a timely manner, match expected losses with investments that mature or become available at appropriate times and help generate income that will contribute to profits. Investment professionals handling insurance assets have an additional complication: Insurers are prohibited by state regulators from investing too heavily in riskier, more volatile instruments. For that reason most insurers are heavily weighted in bonds and similar instruments, and less heavily invested in stocks.

Actuarial: Insurance is based on probability and statistics. Actuaries are skilled in both areas and use their training to help insurers set rates, develop and price policies and coverage, determine reserves for anticipated claims and develop new products that provide coverage at a profit. Actuaries must pass extensive exams to earn their formal designations. Actuaries play influential roles in all sectors of insurance, including property/casualty, life, health and reinsurance. The role of actuaries grows as noninsurance industries—such as hedge funds, risk modelers and capital markets participants—become involved in developing risk products and programs.

Underwriting: At the heart of insurance is the art and science of assuming risk. Underwriters use a combination of data gathering and analysis, interviewing and professional knowledge to evaluate whether a given risk meets the insurer's standards for prudent evaluation. Their job is to evaluate whether given risks can be covered and, if so, under what terms. Underwriting departments often have the authority to accept or reject risks. Perhaps the most significant responsibility of underwriters is to determine premium that recognizes the likelihood of a claim and enables the insurer to earn a profit. Some of the process has been automated, such as when auto and homeowners insurers access information like driving and property records. Applicants for life insurance and some forms of health coverage may be asked to obtain medical evaluations.

Claims: Sometimes called the actual "product" that insurance companies deliver, claims departments usually operate in two areas: at the offices of the insurer and in the field through claims adjusters. Claims are requests for payment based on losses believed by the policyholder to be covered under an insurance policy. Claims personnel evaluate the request and determine the amount of loss the insurer should pay. Requests for claims payment can come directly to insurers or be handled by agents and brokers working directly with the insured. Claims adjusters can work directly for an insurer or operate as independent businesses that can work for multiple insurers. Claims adjusters often have designated levels of authority to settle claims. Adjusters serve as claims investigators and sometimes conduct elaborate investigations in the event of suspected fraudulent claims.

World's Largest Insurance Companies
Based on 2015 nonbanking assets.
(US$ thousands)

2015	2014	Company Name	Country of Domicile		2015 Nonbanking Assets	% Change*
1	1	AXA S.A.	France		921,362,455	6.18
2	2	Allianz SE	Germany		885,115,410	5.84
3	3	MetLife Inc	United States		877,933,000	-2.70
4	5	Prudential Financial Inc	United States		757,388,000	-1.21
5	4	Japan Post Insurance Co., Ltd.	Japan		724,922,808	-3.97
6	7	Nippon Life Insurance Company	Japan		627,704,595	12.70
7	6	Legal & General Group Plc	United Kingdom		588,290,229	-0.69
8	10	Aviva plc	United Kingdom		575,058,114	35.75
9	14	Prudential plc	United Kingdom		573,740,091	4.82
10	8	Berkshire Hathaway Inc.	United States		552,257,000	5.02
11	13	Assicurazioni Generali S.p.A.	Italy		546,949,892	-0.15
12	9	Manulife Financial Corporation	Canada		508,273,089	21.61
13	15	National Mut Ins Fed Agricultural Coop	Japan		501,633,719	3.03
14	12	American International Group, Inc	United States		496,943,000	-3.61
15	11	China Life Insurance (Group) Company	China		466,641,998	10.24
16	19	Aegon N.V.	Netherlands		453,923,971	-2.05
17	16	Dai-ichi Life Insurance Company, Limited	Japan		443,832,530	0.18
18	20	CNP Assurances	France		430,217,188	-0.42
19	17	Ping An Ins (Group) Co of China Ltd	China		418,009,043	20.10
20	18	Zurich Insurance Group Ltd	Switzerland		381,972,000	-6.04
21	23	Credit Agricole Assurances	France		377,033,950	4.79
22	21	Meiji Yasuda Life Insurance Company	Japan		348,170,529	7.07
23	...	Life Insurance Corporation of India	India		331,743,690	8.91
24	25	Munich Reinsurance Company	Germany		302,153,404	1.30
25	24	New York Life Ins Company	United States		301,657,000	7.90

Based on 2015 net premiums written.
(US$ thousands)

2015	2014	Company Name	Country of Domicile		2015 Net Premiums Written	% Change*
1	2	UnitedHealth Group Incorporated[1]	United States		127,163,000	10.29
2	1	AXA S.A.	France		94,958,908	6.06
3	3	Allianz SE	Germany		77,787,128	2.55
4	4	Assicurazioni Generali S.p.A.	Italy		74,795,315	6.46
5	6	Anthem, Inc.	United States		73,051,500	6.31
6	7	China Life Insurance (Group) Company	China		69,666,196	12.06
7	8	Kaiser Foundation Group of Health Plans[2]	United States		67,438,539	7.63
8	10	State Farm Group[2]	United States		64,803,800	2.59
9	5	Nippon Life Insurance Company	Japan		55,650,973	16.59
10	17	Ping An Ins (Group) Co of China Ltd	China		55,603,504	19.57
11	15	National Mut Ins Fed Agricultural Coop	Japan		55,055,005	7.04
12	12	People's Ins Co (Group) of China Ltd	China		55,037,613	12.88
13	11	Aetna Inc.[1]	United States		53,788,800	3.94
14	18	Munich Reinsurance Company	Germany		53,001,414	2.71
15	13	Prudential plc	United Kingdom		52,640,841	10.84
16	9	Humana Inc.[1]	United States		52,409,000	14.03
17	20	Dai-ichi Life Insurance Company, Limited	Japan		49,659,540	2.82
18	16	Japan Post Insurance Co., Ltd.	Japan		47,995,723	-9.24
19	14	Zurich Insurance Group Ltd	Switzerland		42,920,000	-11.83
20	23	Berkshire Hathaway Inc.	United States		42,667,000	0.55
21	22	Life Insurance Corporation of India	India		40,253,278	11.17
22	19	MS&AD Insurance Group Holdings, Inc.	Japan		39,427,737	21.15
23	21	MetLife Inc	United States		38,545,000	-1.34
24	24	American International Group, Inc	United States		37,550,000	-0.83
25	...	Liberty Mutual Holding Company Inc.	United States		34,533,000	0.59

* Percent change is based upon local currency.
1 Premiums shown are earned premiums.
2 A.M. Best consolidation; U.S. companies only.
Source: **BESTLINK**

Insurance Entities

Ownership of traditional insurance companies generally comes in two structures, mutual and stock, although insuring entities may take a number of other forms, including reciprocal exchanges and risk retention groups. Mutual insurers are owned by and run for the benefit of their policyholders. Relative to insurance companies with shareholder ownership, mutual insurers have less access to the capital markets to raise money. Many mutual insurance companies have been formed by people or businesses with a common need, such as farmers. Mutuals pay a return of premium or "policyholder dividend" back to the policyholder if the company has strong financial results and a lower-than-expected number of claims. Policyholders also have the ability to vote on company leadership and have a say in certain corporate governance issues.

Reciprocal insurance companies resemble mutual companies. Whereas a mutual insurance company is incorporated, the reciprocal company is run by a management company, referred to as an attorney-in-fact.

Many mutuals were able to grow during the credit crunch of the late 2000s. Their growth is limited, however, because capital has to be generated internally, as there are no shares to sell. Some top (former) mutual insurance companies, including Metropolitan Life and Prudential, have demutualized to become shareholder-owned

Top 10 U.S. Holding Companies, 2016

Ranked by Assets

Rank	Company Name	AMB#	2016 Total Assets ($000)	2015 Total Assets ($000)	% Change
1	MetLife, Inc.	058175	898,764,000	877,933,000	2.4%
2	Prudential Financial, Inc.	058182	783,962,000	757,255,000	3.5%
3	Berkshire Hathaway Inc.	058334	620,854,000	552,257,000	12.4%
4	American International Group, Inc.	058702	498,264,000	496,842,000	0.3%
5	Lincoln National Corporation	058709	261,627,000	251,908,000	3.9%
6	Principal Financial Group, Inc.	058179	228,014,300	218,660,300	4.3%
7	The Hartford Financial Services Group, Inc.	058707	223,432,000	228,348,000	-2.2%
8	Voya Financial Inc.	050817	214,235,100	218,223,500	-1.8%
9	Pacific Mutual Holding Company	050799	143,298,000	137,184,000	4.5%
10	Ameriprise Financial, Inc.	050542	139,821,000	145,339,000	-3.8%

Ranked by Revenue

Rank	Company Name	AMB#	2016 Total Revenue ($000)	2015 Total Revenue ($000)	% Change
1	Berkshire Hathaway Inc.	058334	223,604,000	210,943,000	6.0%
2	UnitedHealth Group Incorporated	058106	184,840,000	157,107,000	17.7%
3	Anthem, Inc.	058180	84,863,000	79,165,800	7.2%
4	MetLife, Inc.	058175	63,476,000	69,951,000	-9.3%
5	Aetna Inc.	058700	63,155,000	60,337,000	4.7%
6	Prudential Financial, Inc.	058182	58,779,000	57,119,000	2.9%
7	Humana Inc.	058052	54,379,000	54,559,000	-0.3%
8	American International Group, Inc.	058702	52,912,000	58,327,000	-9.3%
9	Centene Corporation	051149	40,721,000	22,795,000	78.6%
10	Cigna Corporation	058703	39,668,000	37,876,000	4.7%

Source: BESTLINK Holding Companies database

BEST

public companies. Typically, demutualization is done to raise capital or expand operations. Other companies, including Pacific Life and Liberty Mutual, took an intermediate step and became part of a mutual holding company structure.

A holding company structure, employed primarily in the United States, provides easier access to the capital markets, whereby shares can be sold to help raise capital. The holding company owns a significant amount, if not all, of another company's or other companies' common stock. Many insurance companies are part of a holding company structure, with the publicly traded parent company owning stock of the subsidiary or the controlled insurance company (or companies).

Captive insurance companies are formed to insure the risks of their parent group or groups, and sometimes will insure risks of the group's customers. Captive insurers have become higher-profile in recent years after many U.S. states and some international jurisdictions adopted legislation and rules encouraging captives to locate in their domiciles.

A risk retention group is a liability insurance company owned by its policyholders. Membership is limited to people in the same business or activity, which exposes them to similar liability risks. The purpose is to assume and spread liability exposure to group members and to provide an alternative risk financing mechanism for liability. These entities are formed under the Liability Risk Retention Act of 1986.

Structural differences between stock and mutual insurance companies affect business decisions. Stock companies have to answer to owners and policyholders, so if management's investment strategies are carried out with shareholder expectations in mind — seizing opportunities for growth and profit — they may be acting at the expense of policyholders. Mutuals, on the other hand, are owned by the policyholders, so the focus likely will be on affordability and dividends.

Observers have struggled to make meaningful comparisons of profitability generated by public and mutual companies. One thing is certain, however: No particular organizational structure is a cure-all for poorly conceived or executed strategies.

Attrition Ahead?

The insurance industry is not immune to job loss and consolidation, even amid a talent shortage. Artificial intelligence, automation and closely managed operations costs could lead to attrition, especially among underwriters, claims adjusters and sales agents, among other positions, as the industry evolves.

Carriers' Job Gains and Losses

What positions are projected for job growth and loss in the insurance industry from 2014 to 2024.

▼	**2.3%**	Claims adjusters, examiners and investigators
▼	**0.3%**	Insurance sales agents
▼	**15.5%**	Underwriters
▼	**7.8%**	Carriers' auto damage appraisers
▲	**21.8%**	Mathematical science workers
▲	**42.7%**	Statisticians
▲	**30.2%**	Operations research analysts
▲	**12.7%**	Actuaries
▲	**14.7%**	Computer and mathematics occupations
▲	**33.5%**	Information security analysts
▲	**21.7%**	Web developers
▲	**22.7%**	Software developers, applications

Source: Source: Bureau of Labor Statistics

"Automation will gobble up positions," said Monica Ningen, head of property underwriting in the United States and Canada for Swiss Re. "I don't think many of them completely go away, but change. The companies are going to find far more efficient ways."

The headwinds of the past decade have taken their toll. The low interest rate environment has produced lackluster investment yields. There have been disappointing underwriting results. Several sectors are awash in overcapacity.

Mergers and acquisitions are on the rise as companies seek growth. Some have conducted layoffs since the start of 2016, such as American International Group, Liberty Mutual and MassMutual. In 2017, Lloyd's announced potential job cuts.

These pressures have contributed to insurers' adoption of automation and artificial intelligence. The aim is to reduce administrative costs—which account for about 30% of premium paid, experts say—and duplicated work while increasing efficiency, which often results in staff cuts.

It may even be the beginning of some familiar positions vanishing permanently. "The less complex jobs, the more routine jobs can be replaced by artificial intelligence, automation and computer technology enhancements," said Joyce Dunn, vice president at The Jacobson Group.

Automation will be the primary reason for staff reductions

through the middle of 2018, 16% of companies reported in the Jacobson Group and Ward Group Insurance Labor Market Study. Insurers invested more than $500 million in 2016 in artificial intelligence, according to Accenture.

Increased use of automation, artificial intelligence, outsourcing and block chain/distributed ledger technology as well as growing direct-to-consumer online sales threaten underwriters, claims personnel, sales reps, payment processors, administrative support and operations staff and eventually, even IT workers.

Three of the top five occupations by size employed by insurance carriers are projected to lose employment from 2014 to 2024, according to the Bureau of Labor Statistics: claims adjusters, examiners and investigators, insurance sales agents and underwriters.

"Automation and productivity-enhancing technology is really the story for these occupations that have just been dropping in the last number of years and are projected to continue to lose occupations," said Frankie Velez, a BLS bureau chief of occupational outlook studies, referring to the 2014-2024 projections. "And for the jobs that remain, it seems some of the qualifications have changed because they're doing more complicated work."

Insurance companies will spend $90 million on average on artificial intelligence technologies by 2020, according to Tata Consultancy Services.

About two-thirds of insurers already use artificial intelligence-based "virtual assistants," consulting firm Accenture reported in April 2017. The number will rise. A majority of companies said they plan to invest "significantly" in AI in the next three years.

Artificial intelligence remains in its infancy in the industry, used mostly as chatbots to communicate with customers and to improve data processing. But it will be employed more frequently. It soon will address inquiries about the statuses of claims and bills, traditionally handled by call centers, according to Accenture.

Fukoku Mutual Life Insurance laid off 34 employees early in 2017, some 30% of its claims staff, replacing them with an artificial intelligence system that can calculate payouts to policyholders.

In May 2017, Zurich announced it was employing AI to handle personal injury claims and planned to expand its use.

However, only 5% of all jobs can be entirely automated, according to McKinsey and Co. And automation cannot replace the qualitative judgment necessary for effective underwriting, PwC's *Top Insurance Industry Issues in 2016* report said. Even if abundant attrition does occur, it is not nearly enough to stave off the looming talent gap. Underwriters, actuaries, adjusters "and folks who have to do critical thinking and decision-making that is really quite nuanced" will not be fully automated—at least not for decades, said Keith Wolfe, president of U.S. property/casualty, regional and national, for Swiss Re.

By Jeff Roberts

BEST

Property/Casualty Market at a Glance

Property/casualty is known as "nonlife" insurance in many parts of the world. The word "property" usually refers to physical things, including autos, buildings, ships and other concrete items that can be lost, damaged or otherwise become a financial loss to the insured. The word "casualty" usually refers to the concept of liability, and is often associated with coverage of negligent acts or omissions. Casualty areas are some of the largest, including auto liability, professional liability, workers' compensation and general liability. The relative size of property/casualty insurers is often gauged by premiums collected.

In the United States, property/casualty insurers file a special statement with the National Association of Insurance Commissioners. The filing is designed to determine premiums and losses by lines of business and to give an accurate view of the insurer's reserving for loss.

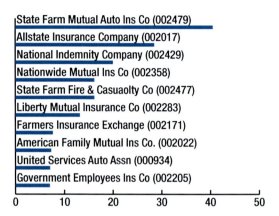

**U.S. Property/Casualty –
Top Insurers by Net Premiums Written (2016)**
(US$ billions)

State Farm Mutual Auto Ins Co (002479)
Allstate Insurance Company (002017)
National Indemnity Company (002429)
Nationwide Mutual Ins Co (002358)
State Farm Fire & Casuaolty Co (002477)
Liberty Mutual Insurance Co (002283)
Farmers Insurance Exchange (002171)
American Family Mutual Ins Co. (002022)
United Services Auto Assn (000934)
Government Employees Ins Co (002205)

0   10   20   30   40   50

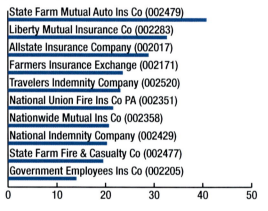

**U.S. Property/Casualty –
Top Insurers by Gross Premiums Written (2016)**
(US$ billions)

State Farm Mutual Auto Ins Co (002479)
Liberty Mutual Insurance Co (002283)
Allstate Insurance Company (002017)
Farmers Insurance Exchange (002171)
Travelers Indemnity Company (002520)
National Union Fire Ins Co PA (002351)
Nationwide Mutual Ins Co (002358)
National Indemnity Company (002429)
State Farm Fire & Casualty Co (002477)
Government Employees Ins Co (002205)

0   10   20   30   40   50

Source: **BESTLINK** – Aggregates & Averages
Property/Casualty United States & Canada, 2017 Edition

As of this publication, A.M. Best's database contained filing statements for 2,631 total single companies operating in the U.S. property/casualty market. According to the U.S. Department of Labor, 570,800 people work in the property/casualty industry.

According to A.M. Best's annual *Review & Preview* report, the property/casualty industry faces several issues.

Abundant capital continues to be both a benefit and a challenge to the industry. The investments that consistently generate the bulk of the industry's operating income also provide the cushion of capital that allow competitive conditions to first creep, then gallop, back into the market.

U.S. Property/Casualty – Top Insurers by Total Admitted Assets (2016)
(US$ billions)

National Indemnity Company (002429)			
State Farm Mutual Auto Ins Co (002479)			
Allstate Insurance Company (002017)			
Liberty Mutual Insurance Co (002283)			
Continental Casualty Company (002128)			
State Farm Fire & Casualty Co (002477)			
Nationwide Mutual Ins Co (002358)			
United Services Auto Assn (000934)			
Zurich American Insurance Co (002563)			
American Home Assurance Co (002034)			

0   50   100   150   200

U.S. Property/Casualty – Top Insurers by Policyholder Surplus (2016)
(US$ billions)

National Indemnity Company (002429)			
State Farm Mutual Auto Ins Co (002479)			
United Services Auto Assn (000934)			
Liberty Mutual Insurance Co (002283)			
State Farm Fire & Casualty Co (002477)			
Government Employees Ins Co (002205)			
Allstate Insurance Company (002017)			
Columbia Insurance Company (004330)			
Nationwide Mutual Ins Co (002358)			
Hartford Fire Insurance Co (002231)			

0   20   40   60   80   100   120

Source: **BESTLINK** – *Aggregates & Averages*
Property/Casualty United States & Canada, 2017 Edition

U.S. Property/Casualty – Direct Premiums Written
(US$ billions)

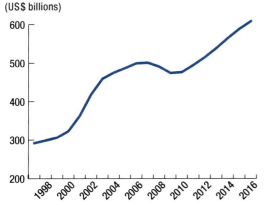

Source: **BESTLINK** – *Aggregates & Averages*
Property/Casualty United States & Canada, 2017 Edition

Personal Lines

In personal lines, use of data to stratify customers into ever more targeted price groups, and to focus marketing to those groups, is now expected. Companies that have not effectively adopted these technologies find themselves adversely selected against. Size does not provide immunity from the realities of the personal lines arms race. The use of these technologies has spread beyond personal lines underwriting. For example, it is used to triage incoming claims to ensure that they are routed promptly to adjusters with specialized training or special investigative units, and into commercial lines.

Among commercial lines companies, use of data and analytics to determine technical price at a risk level has become critical in maintaining underwriting discipline as conditions have deteriorated.

Catastrophe losses, including hurricanes, wildfires, hail and other perils, are always an issue, as are expected increases in interest rates. To the extent that both move up gradually, pricing and investment income will likely increase at a rate that will allow the industry to keep pace with rising inflation. However, with the industry in a downward period in the pricing cycle, an increase in the inflation rate could cause a sharp contraction in profitability.

Emerging Risks

The industry is contending with other emerging issues such as cyber exposures, both in terms of providing coverage, as well as mitigating the industry's own exposure:

BEST

• The changing face of global terrorism, its intersection with cyber exposures and the potential impact on physical and financial exposure; and

• The evolution of driverless vehicle technology, which may prove to have more immediate applications for commercial auto than personal auto.

Risks are emerging from around the globe, insurers and researchers have told *Best's Review*, A.M. BestTV and A.M. Best Radio. Fredrik Finnman, group risk insurance manager for lock manufacturer Assa Abloy, based in Sweden, said even lock makers face growing electronic exposure. That's because the lock industry has spent the better part of a decade focusing on moving locks from physical controls to digital controls, typically used in hotels and commercial facilities. "With that comes different types of product liability risk," Finnman said. "Naturally, just as with other type of operations, we face the risk of hacker attacks on these cyber systems."

Thomas Varney, Allianz, said an annual survey showed that concern about business interruption risks remains paramount among risk managers, brokers and experts. But the nature of that risk is changing, from one based around physical events such as catastrophes, to concerns over cyber intrusion, market disruption and political risks that would hamper the supply chain.

Michael Tanenbaum, Chubb, points to social engineering fraud as a burgeoning risk. That includes email scams and other outreaches to senior management that leads to transfers of money or opens the door to ransomware attacks.

Philip Rocace, Cyence, said models of cyber must incorporate expectations and frailties of human behavior. One growing risk is "silent cyber," in which insurers may be responsible for coverage because it was never directly addressed or excluded in policies.

David Loughran, Praedicat, said the firm's mining of scientific literature shows that endocrine disruptors, chemicals found in many plastic products that have migrated into the environment, could become larger issues as medical research uncovers more effects.

The biggest risk of cyber is that it may be beyond the insurance industry's ability to underwrite it. "One of the issues we have in the industry is we've got a lot of policies which are silent on cyber," Stephen Catlin, executive deputy chairman, XL Catlin said. "Question marks: Are they carrying cyber or are they not? How will an American court feel about that in the event of a major cyber catastrophe? I don't think, in fact I know, that the industry, we cannot pay for the potential cyber loss that could happen in the globe. It's not within our ability," Catlin said. "Can we actually honor the promise that we've made to people for cyber?"

Property/Casualty Coverage Types And Lines of Business

U.S. Property/Casualty – Direct Premiums Written by Line of Business (2016)
(US$ thousands)

	No of Cos.	Direct Premiums Written
Fire	1,011	12,657,640
Allied Lines	929	10,805,547
Multi Peril Crop	43	9,293,535
Federal Flood	140	2,875,086
Private Crop	37	1,046,344
Federal Flood	53	412,618
Farmowners M.P.	209	4,128,368
Homeowners M.P.	880	90,794,538
Comm. M.P.-Non-Liab.	767	25,264,192
Comm. M.P.-Liability	715	14,667,643
Mortgage Guaranty	20	4,932,781
Ocean Marine	190	3,397,858
Inland Marine	1,030	21,310,836
Financia Guaranty	15	455,797
Medical Prof. Liab.	324	9,054,877
Earthquake	537	2,209,574
Group A&H	102	4,666,891
Credit A&H	10	172,749
Other A&H	94	1,705,111
Workers' Comp.	709	58,255,242
Other Liab.-Occ	1,301	40,968,374
Oth Liab-Claims-Made	607	21,273,288
Excess WC	61	1,189,274
Products Liability	482	3,555,498
Pvt Pass Auto Liab.	861	127,815,201
Comm'l Auto Liab.	873	25,122,938
Pvt Pass Auto P.D.	866	85,895,581
Comm'l Auto P.D.	800	8,006,291
Aircraft	73	1,586,636
Fidelity	289	1,256,881
Surety	342	5,894,410
Burglary & Theft	413	298,250
Boiler & Mach.	390	1,719,328
Credit	108	1,962,810
International	5	64,725
Warranty	61	2,909,565
Other Lines	113	1,202,626

Source: BESTLINK – Aggregates & Averages Property/Casualty U.S. & Canada, 2017 Edition

Property insurance covers damages or loss of property. As a result, rates can be significantly higher in areas susceptible to perils such as hurricanes. Casualty insurance covers indemnity losses and legal expenses from losses such as bodily injury or damage that the policyholder may cause to others.

When a loss occurs, insurance companies establish a claim reserve for the amount of the expected cost of the claim using a projection of estimated loss costs over a period of time. While property reserves are established when a property loss occurs and are usually settled soon after a loss, casualty reserves are established for losses that may not be paid or settled for years (i.e. medical professional liability, workers' compensation, production liability and environmental-related claims). These "long-tail" lines of business are so named because of the length of time that may elapse before claims are finally settled.

Determining and comparing profitability among property/casualty companies typically is achieved through the combined ratio, which measures the percentage of claims and expenses incurred relative to premiums earned/written. A combined ratio of less than 100 means that the insurer is making an underwriting profit. Companies with combined ratios over 100 still may earn an operating profit, however, because the ratio does not account for investment income.

Property/casualty insurance generally falls into two areas of concentration: personal and commercial lines.

The two largest product lines within the personal lines sector are auto insurance and homeowners insurance.

Commercial lines include insurance for businesses, professionals and commercial establishments. There are many more varieties of commercial lines products than personal lines. The largest two lines are workers' compensation and other liability.

Personal Lines of Business

Personal insurance protects families, individuals and their property, typically homes and vehicles, from loss and damage. Auto and homeowners coverage dominates mostly because of legal provisions that mandate coverage be obtained.

Auto: The largest line of business in the property/casualty sector is auto insurance. According to A.M. Best's BestLink database, the top 50 groups writing auto insurance captured 87% of the total market in 2016, or $201 billion of the $230 billion for all U.S. auto coverage. The largest writer of U.S. private passenger auto, and all auto coverage overall, remains State Farm Group.

Auto insurance includes collision, liability, comprehensive, personal injury protection and coverage in the event another motorist is uninsured or underinsured.

Homeowners: The second-largest line of personal property/casualty insurance is homeowners, representing $90.8 billion in direct premiums written for the U.S. property/casualty industry in 2016. Historically, the leading cause of U.S. insured catastrophe losses has been hurricanes and tropical storms, followed by severe thunderstorms and winter storms. The top 25 groups writing homeowners multiperil coverage represented 75% of the U.S. market for homeowners coverage, according to A.M. Best's BestLink database. The largest writer of homeowners multiperil coverage is also State Farm Group.

Commercial Lines of Business

Commercial insurance protects businesses, hospitals, governments, schools and other organizations from losses.

Two of the top lines in the commercial segment are workers' compensation and general liability.

Workers' Compensation: Insurers on behalf of employers pay benefits regardless of who is to blame for a work-related injury or accident, unless the employee was negligent. In return, the employee gives up the right to sue.

General Liability: General liability insurance protects business owners (the "insured") from the risks of liabilities imposed by lawsuits and similar claims. Liability insurance is designed to offer its insureds specific protection against third-party insurance claims; in other words, payment is not typically made to the insured, but rather to someone suffering loss who is not a party to the insurance contract. In general, damages caused by intentional acts are not covered under general liability insurance policies. When a claim is made, the insurance carrier has the duty to defend the insured.

Other major lines of business in the property/casualty commercial sector include:

Aircraft (all perils): Aircraft coverage is often excluded under standard commercial general liability forms. Coverage for aircraft liability loss exposure can include hull (physical damage) and medical payments coverages.

Allied Lines: Coverage for loss of or damage to real or personal property by reason other than fire. Losses from wind and hail, water (sprinkler, flood, rain), civil disorder and damage by aircraft or vehicles are included.

Boiler and Machinery: Coverage for damage to boilers, pressure vessels and machinery.

Burglary and Theft: Coverage to protect property from burglary, theft, forgery, counterfeiting, fraud and the like. Protection can include on- and off-premises exposure.

Commercial Auto: Coverage that protects against financial loss because of legal liability for injury to persons or damage to property of others caused by the insured's motor vehicle.

Commercial Multiple Peril: Commercial insurance coverage combining two or more property, liability and/or risk exposures.

Fidelity: Coverage for employee theft of money, securities or property, written with a per loss limit, a per employee limit or a per position limit. Employee dishonesty coverage is one of the key coverages provided in a commercial crime policy.

Financial Guaranty: Credit protection for investors in municipal bonds, commercial mortgage-backed securities and auto or student loans. Provides financial recourse in the event of a default on the bond or other instrument.

Fire: Coverage for loss of or damage to real or personal property due to fire or lightning. Losses from interruption of business and loss of other income from these sources are included.

Inland Marine: Coverage for goods in transit and goods, such as construction equipment, subject to frequent relocation.

Medical Professional Liability: Protects against failure to use due care and the standard of care expected from a doctor, dentist, nurse, hospital or other health-related organization. Covers bodily injury or property damage as well as liability for personal injury.

Mortgage Guaranty: Insurance against financial loss because of nonpayment of principal, interest and other amounts agreed to be paid under the terms of a note, bond or other evidence of indebtedness that is secured by real estate.

Multiple Peril Crop: Protects against losses caused by crop yields that are too low. This line was developed initially by the U.S. Department of Agriculture.

Ocean Marine: Provides protection for all types of oceangoing vessels and their cargo as well as legal liability of owners and shippers.

Products Liability: Protection against loss arising out of legal liability because of injury or damage resulting from the use of a product or the liability of a contractor after a job is completed.

Surety: The surety bond guarantees that the principal of a bond will perform its obligations.

Changing Drivers: How Ride Hailing Is Changing Insurance

A seismic change has come to America's roadways. The sharing economy has spawned a new landscape: on-demand, peer-to-peer transportation networks. The paradigm shift has redefined how commuters, tourists and others view local travel, especially in metropolitan centers and college towns.

The growing appeal and convenience of auto-sharing mobile apps has created a need for a new kind of insurance. It also is forcing the industry to adapt not only its products, but the way it views the landscape. On-demand transportation has blurred, and in some cases, erased the line separating personal lines and commercial activity. It is a disruptor that has altered the way property/casualty insurers have operated since their inception.

Ride hailing (aka ride sharing) has been called the early success story of shared mobility. More than a dozen insurers offer products. Legislation has passed in most states establishing coverage standards and regulating transportation network companies (TNC). That clarity has enabled carriers to expand product offerings even further.

But shared mobility has developed well beyond peer-to-peer ride hailing. Car sharing and carpooling participation is on the rise. On-demand food, grocery and package delivery is becoming a huge growth area, experts say. And ride hailing is becoming a vital piece of the mass transit infrastructure in some metropolitan areas.

Local governments and transit systems are partnering with TNCs to subsidize rides to broaden public transportation options.

Insurers are adjusting to a rapidly growing marketplace, even if they are still catching up with the evolving phenomenon, experts say.

"What we're seeing is this on-demand economy, ride sharing, car sharing, is going to materially change the way we think about product, underwriting and rating," said John Matley, a principal in Deloitte Consulting's insurance and technology practices. "It's not just a product challenge, but the processes and technology that's behind it.

"Insurers are going to have to get flexible and break down the barriers between what they traditionally think of as commercial lines and personal lines. It's not as simple as it's been for 100 years. We believe we'll see the car sharing and ride sharing total miles increase pretty dramatically. Vehicle usage

John Matley

is changing, and the insurance is going to need to evolve with that."

The concept is both old and startlingly new. Familiar services—taxis, car rental, package delivery—are being provided in a fresh and innovative way.

Shared mobility is fueled by the same engine that's driving the entire sharing economy: on-demand service in a peer-to-peer marketplace where technology and personal assets are leveraged to meet emerging customer needs.

Each sector presents insurers with an opportunity to evolve and grow. Coverage has to change with those emerging needs, experts say. Carriers will have to revise products and pricing as the demand for flexibility increases. They potentially will have to devise hybrid offerings that straddle personal and commercial driving. And they will need to shift to usage-based products harnessing telematics data.

The old models of six-month or annual policies and strict commercial/personal divisions may no longer apply as drivers operate vehicles for different platforms and even different on-demand segments all in the same day.

"It's the power of the smartphone to call a car to take me where I want to go. It's now the power of the smartphone to summon food or order a package and have it delivered to my house in less than an hour," said Randy Nornes, an executive vice president for Aon Risk Solutions. "On demand is the big theme. Making an on-demand system work requires a different insurance mindset, including new products and regulatory framework.

"It's actually creating a network that will go anywhere, anytime. The industry's opportunity is to look at this as a huge growth area and to create products to basically follow the growth. This is one of the biggest growth stories out there for the entire economy."

Insurers continue to figure out where they fit in this new world. "I view it as just the beginning," said Dave Border, Allstate's senior vice president of emerging businesses. "I think the transformation of vehicle ownership and the paradigm shift of a person owning a car and driving it for their own purpose has begun. It's hard to predict where the end of the transformation will be of how people drive and use their vehicles.

"Everything has become a hybrid blend of personal and commercial. The real threat is not adapting and falling behind the market."

The pace of change for insurers is accelerating. Shared mobility is "only just starting to dent" the marketplace, Matley said. Global car-sharing revenue will climb to $6.5 billion by 2024, an increase from $1.1 billion in 2015, according to Navigant Research. Less than 2% of the 3.7 trillion total miles driven annually in the United States (2014 figures) is ride share, car share or taxi mileage. And only 15% of Americans have used a ride-hailing app, according to a Pew Research Center report.
But that will soon change. More than 60% of the 4.8 trillion annual miles predicted to be driven by 2040 will be in ride sharing/car sharing, Deloitte forecasts.

By Jeff Roberts

Insuring the Uninsurable

As he read a report on global natural catastrophe losses, Jamie Miller of Swiss Re was not surprised by the discrepancy between insured and economic losses. And, yet, he was stunned by it.

"It still confounds me that year in and year out, the percentage of insured losses almost never changes," said Miller, head of North America property and specialty lines for Swiss Re Corporate Solutions.

Nearly three-quarters of disaster-related losses were uninsured in 2016, according to Aon Benfield. While it would be easy to dismiss that statistic as being driven by lack of insurance participation in emerging markets, consider this: 70% of losses from Hurricane Matthew, which hit the southeastern U.S. and Caribbean in 2016, were uninsured.

"Even in the most advanced insurance markets in the world, there are still big gaps of exposure for clients," Miller said.

Insurers are searching for innovative ways to fill those gaps, and parametric insurance products are one of the solutions they're using. Parametric insurance products are an increasingly popular way to plug some of the holes that traditional policies haven't covered—from deductible payments to over-limit losses to lost tax revenues.

These innovative solutions have come from new entrants, established players and even insureds themselves. Startups such as New Paradigm Underwriters and Assured Risk Cover have entered the market with supplemental coverages. At the same

time, industry giants such as Swiss Re have responded to insureds' needs with parametric insurance products such as STORM and QUAKE.

"If you can figure out a parameter that you can measure and tie it back to loss experience of some sort, then you can create parametric coverage," said Ben Brookes, vice president of capital markets for RMS. "That's exactly what's happening in the industry."

While some of the most well-known parametric insurance solutions, including the African Risk Capacity, were designed for regions of the world where underwriting data was scarce, the concept is taking off in developed markets for the precise opposite reason—the abundance of data.

"We're importing that concept into advanced markets like the United States," said Alex Kaplan, senior vice president of global partnerships at Swiss Re. "What

Alok Jha

was a fairly blunt instrument maybe 15 years ago is now becoming incredibly honed because of the various data sources we have."

As more data becomes available, experts say the potential for new parametric insurance solutions is vast. While the first wave has been around natural catastrophe-related products, the expectation is that solutions could broaden to cover perils such as cyber and expand into areas such as contingent business interruption.

"Because you have this great surge of data sources, you could see a time in the future where every single street lamp in a city has an anemometer in it with a wind gauge or a rain gauge in it," Kaplan said. "It sends data immediately to an insurer who has otherwise insured a small business. Because there was a cloud burst and it rained for half a day, the coffee shop on the corner saw a massive drop in customer activity. The insurer could instantaneously transfer the potential lost revenue as a result of that rainstorm directly onto their mobile phone. You could see that scenario occurring at some point."

Daniel Stander, managing director of RMS, said all of the technological tools are in place to grow this market.

"The data is out there to build parametric products," Stander said. "The know-how is out there to design parametric triggers. The capital is out there to provide parametric covers. From a technical standpoint, there is nothing stopping this."

Stander said innovation in the market is driven as much by insurers as it is by insureds.

"Of course we're seeing the industry lead," he said. "Equally the industry is responding to innovative requests from insureds—be they large corporate insureds or large public insureds, namely governments. For the first time, we're seeing the public sector grasp the idea that unless they can measure their risk properly, they're unable to manage it effectively. That's where these conversations are starting. Not with a request for risk financing, but with a desire to understand exposure and risk. Insurance is then responding to that, and innovative insurance products are a response to that underlying need.

"For the first time in my career, insurance is suddenly very, very fashionable. There is a lot of desire at all levels of government to engage with risk analytics deeply. The conversations are already happening in collaboration: government, modeler and, where appropriate, risk capital provider."

Peace of Mind

Assured Risk Cover (ARC), a California-based startup, launched StormPeace, a parametric insurance product that offers hurricane coverage for Florida homeowners. It developed from ARC co-founder Alok Jha's desire to give back to society. StormPeace policies pay out immediately after a hurricane, bridging the gap between when the damage occurs and when a homeowner's insurance claim pays out.

By Kate Smith

Life Insurers Search For New Models, Technology

A.M. Best's annual *Review & Preview* report details a range of issues facing the life/annuity sectors.

Premium growth for the life and annuity industry has been challenged in recent years due to a number of different factors, including the industry's mature status, difficulties in updating and improving distribution capabilities in order to penetrate the underserved middle market and millennial populations, and an increasingly complex and evolving regulatory environment. Additionally, the low interest rate and competitive market environments have been major contributors to the sub-par premium growth experienced during this time.

Top 10 U.S. Life/Health Companies
Ranked by 2016 Gross Premiums Written

(US$ thousands)

Rank	Company Name	AMB#	GPW
1	Metropolitan Life Ins Co	006704	90,839,157
2	UnitedHealthcare Ins Co	008290	45,779,677
3	Prudential Ins Co of America	006974	36,880,072
4	Principal Life Insurance Co	006150	30,083,331
5	Aetna Life Ins Co	006006	27,613,879
6	Massachusetts Mutual Life Ins	06695	26,877,935
7	Hannover Life Reassurance Amer	68031	23,533,342
8	Jackson National Life Ins Co	06596	22,283,786
9	AXA Equitable Life Ins Co	06341	21,681,478
10	John Hancock Life Ins Co USA	006681	21,356,342

Top 10 U.S. Life/Health Companies
Ranked by 2016 Net Premiums Written

(US$ thousands)

Rank	Company Name	AMB#	NPW
1	UnitedHealthcare Ins Co	008290	44,379,154
2	Prudential Ins Co of America	006974	25,550,197
3	Metropolitan Life Ins Co	06704	24,891,230
4	Massachusetts Mutual Life Ins	006695	21,408,423
5	American Fam Assur Columbus	06051	18,902,763
6	Jackson National Life Ins Co	006596	18,631,372
7	Aetna Life Ins Co	006006	18,556,444
8	Northwestern Mutual Life Ins	06845	17,660,628
9	Lincoln National Life Ins Co	006664	17,172,036
10	Prudential Annuities Life Assr	008715	15,511,697

Top 10 U.S. Life/Health Companies
Ranked by 2016 Total Admitted Assets

(US$ thousands)

Rank	Company Name	AMB#	Admitted Assets
1	Metropolitan Life Ins Co	006704	396,366,830
2	Teachers Ins & Annuity Assoc	007112	282,442,386
3	Prudential Ins Co of America	006974	260,294,334
4	Northwestern Mutual Life Ins	006845	250,507,191
5	John Hancock Life Ins Co USA	006681	229,892,290
6	Massachusetts Mutual Life Ins	006695	223,670,466
7	Lincoln National Life Ins Co	006664	221,258,928
8	Jackson National Life Ins Co	006596	204,781,179
9	AXA Equitable Life Ins Co	006341	174,067,924
10	Principal Life Insurance Co	006150	171,337,718

Top 10 U.S. Life/Health Companies
Ranked by 2016 Capital & Surplus

(US$ thousands)

Rank	Company Name	AMB#	Capital & Surplus
1	Teachers Ins & Annuity Assoc	007112	35,583,089
2	Northwestern Mutual Life Ins	006845	20,229,584
3	New York Life Ins Co	006820	20,107,561
4	Massachusetts Mutual Life Ins	006695	15,423,490
5	AGC Life Insurance Company	009199	12,311,211
6	American Fam Assur Columbus	006051	11,221,055
7	Metropolitan Life Ins Co	006704	11,194,820
8	Prudential Ins Co of America	006974	11,173,696
9	State Farm Life Ins Co	007080	10,177,270
10	American General Life Ins Co	006058	9,000,520

Source: **BESTLINK**, A.M. Best data.

Insurers have implemented a number of strategies in response to these market challenges, including focusing on distribution and compensation structures, divesting/ exiting more capital-intensive product lines, and utilizing technology to improve market penetration and customer retention. Other industry responses have included focusing on less interest-sensitive businesses such as fee-based asset management, developing product partnerships and introducing new innovative and simplified product features and riders, in an effort to drive product brand.

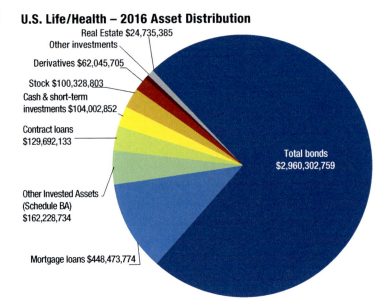

U.S. Life/Health – 2016 Asset Distribution

Real Estate $24,735,385
Other investments
Derivatives $62,045,705
Stock $100,328,803
Cash & short-term investments $104,002,852
Contract loans $129,692,133
Other Invested Assets (Schedule BA) $162,228,734
Mortgage loans $448,473,774
Total bonds $2,960,302,759

Source: BESTLINK – *Aggregates & Averages Life/Health U.S. & Canada 2017 Edition* Securities are reported on the basis prescribed by the National Association of Insurance Commissioners.

Product pivoting has been successful in maintaining sales levels but not always for growing them as the industry still struggles with muted consumer demand.

Developing Issues

Distribution has been an important tool that has helped insurers penetrate and thrive in very competitive markets. Domestic insurers are starting to see distribution competition through new channels such as affinity groups, retailers and online comparison platforms.

Non-traditional online competitors such as Amazon and Google continue to remain a threat either as a direct distributor or manufacturer of insurance products, or simply by providing access to their vast client bases.

While some insurers use some form of direct-to-consumer and retailer-based marketing, insurance companies that do not access non-affiliated retailers and/or online marketing services will be at a competitive disadvantage.

New technology is crucial in order to reach millennials, the middle-market and consumers' appetite for more flexible and convenient interaction. Although the challenge lies in the increased up-front expenses it takes to develop improved tools and workflow with the hopes of lower expenses following implementation, companies have been making these investments with the longer-term view in mind. This also creates a more competitive marketplace as smaller and more nimble companies without the burden of legacy systems and processes may be able to adapt to change easier and faster.

Organizations with a strong financial capacity have a greater ability to invest in their career agency sales force, along with continuous hiring and training that goes along with maintaining this distribution channel.

There is broad consensus that distribution systems for the life insurance industry must undergo a rapid, strategic evolution based on changing demographic and macroeconomic conditions. The structure of basic customer relationships, the core value propositions of the products, and the role agents will play as the distribution models expand and diversify are all ripe for change.

Despite the headwinds of low interest rates, tepid economic growth and intense competition within the employee benefits marketplace, many insurance carriers have renewed their focus on growing this business segment over the past several years. This can be attributable to the less capital intensive and volatile nature of many group life and accident & health products compared with other more interest-sensitive product lines.

Life Market at a Glance

Life/health insurers cover the risks of dying, offer retirement savings products and provide a variety of protections against disability, specific types of illness and more. As of this publication, A.M. Best's database contained annual filings for 771 single combined life/health companies operating in the United States. According to the U.S. Department of Labor, 351,700 people work in the U.S. life insurance sector. Life insurers often have longer investment and coverage horizons because retirement and mortality are often events that are decades away. The relative size of life/health insurers is often gauged by assets under management. Life insurers have increasingly embraced annuities and other forms of retirement savings, as sales of traditional life products have been flat or grown modestly and baby boomers transition into retirement.

The U.S. life/health industry collected $606 billion in premium income and had $6.8 trillion in total assets as of 2016, the most recent full year available. The largest lines of business as measured by premium income, in order, are individual annuities, group annuities and ordinary life. Other lines of business include supplemental contracts, credit life, group life, industrial life, group accident & health, credit accident & health and other accident & health.

According to the 2017 edition of *Best's Key Rating Guide - Life/Health, United States and Canada*, Metropolitan Life Ins. Co. leads the list of largest life/annuity companies ranked by total admitted assets, with $396 billion in total admitted assets as of year-end 2016 (in 2017 MetLife separated its U.S. retail business, a move that could affect future rankings.

EXPECT BIG THINGS®
FROM APPLIED UNDERWRITERS

Expect big things in workers' compensation. Most classes approved, nationwide. It pays to get a quote from Applied.® For information call (877) 234-4450 or visit auw.com/us. Follow us at bigdoghq.com.

APPLIED®
UNDERWRITERS

Risk Profile

The risk profile of life insurance is very different from that of property/casualty insurance. Life insurance is generally more asset intensive, and most product liabilities have a substantially longer duration.

The main purpose of life insurance is to cover the risk of dying too early or, in the case of annuities, the risks that may come with living longer than expected. Policies help beneficiaries maintain their standard of living after the policyholder dies. They also can protect beneficiaries and insureds from the possibility of outliving their assets.

While some types of life insurance include a savings component that can provide retirement income, life insurance itself isn't necessarily an investment. But for insurance companies, and especially life insurers, profitability is largely dependent on investment performance. In general, life insurers have enough data surrounding life expectancies and risk classes to determine rates and to accurately predict claims.

Because a policy can remain in effect for decades, life insurers' obligations tend to be relatively long-term. As a result, many insurers invest in longer-duration assets such as long-term bonds and real estate. The current low interest rate environment has put increased pressure on life insurers' investment portfolios.

Important Lines of Life Business and Products

Life insurers market a variety of life products that range from simple to complex.

Total Life, In Force & Issued: The size of a life company can be measured by the face amount of its portfolio — that is, the amount of life insurance it has issued as well as the amount in force. In force is the total face amount of insurance outstanding at a point in time. Issued measures the face amount of policies an insurer has sold within a given time period.

Permanent Life: Permanent life provides death benefits and cash value in return for periodic payments. Cash surrender value, or nonforfeiture value, is the sum of money an insurance company will

Top 10 Global Life Reinsurance Groups
Ranked by Unaffiliated Gross Premiums Written in 2016
(USD Millions)

2017 Ranking	Company Name	Life Only Gross	Net	Total Shareholders' Funds
1	Munich Reinsurance Company	$14,370	$13,960	$33,493
2	Swiss Re Ltd.	$13,744	$12,140	$35,716
3	Reinsurance Group of America Inc.	$10,107	$9,249	$7,093
4	SCOR S.E.	$8,627	$7,915	$7,055
5	Hannover Rück S.E.	$7,533	$6,778	$10,264
6	Great West Lifeco	$6,195	$6,112	$13,857
7	Berkshire Hathaway Inc.	$4,672	$4,672	$286,359
8	Pacific LifeCorp	$1,570	$1,172	$11,140
9	PartnerRe Ltd.	$1,168	$1,117	$6,688
10	Assicurazioni Generali SpA	$1,145	$1,145	$27,047

Note: See Top 50 World's Largest Reinsurance Groups ranking for any related footnotes.
Source: A.M. Best data and research

pay a policyholder if he or she decides to cancel the policy before it expires or before he or she dies. Over the long term, these products usually produce solid, sustainable profitability that is derived from adequate pricing, underwriting and investment returns. Permanent life products include whole life, universal life and variable universal life.

Whole Life: Pays a death benefit and also accumulates a cash value. These have a high initial expense strain for the issuing company due to large first-year commissions to agents as a percentage of premiums. Over time, whole life provides an income stream to the company and the agent. It carries premium, death benefit and cash value guarantees that other products don't provide.

Universal Life: These are flexible premium policies that incorporate a savings element. The cash values that are accumulated are put into investments with the intention of earning more in interest. Those accumulations can be used to reduce later premiums, or to build up the cash value. For companies offering this product, the premium payment flexibility adds an element of uncertainty, as does the potential for changing market conditions that can affect interest rates. The next generation of this product line, universal life with secondary guarantees, offers competitive rates while providing long-term premium and death benefit guarantees, regardless of actual performance. The tight pricing and high reserve requirements can limit profitability.

Variable Universal Life: These flexible premium policies allow for investments of the cash value into mutual-fund-like accounts the insurance carrier holds in separate accounts rather than in its general account. Because policy values will vary based on the performance of investments, these policies present an investment risk to the policyholder. Rather than having a monthly addition to the cash value based upon a declared interest-crediting rate, the accumulated cash value of the variable policy is adjusted daily to reflect the investment experience of the funds selected. Insurers can be susceptible to profit fluctuations because of the equity market's effect on mutual fund fees. In addition, the insurer lacks control over separate-account assets, and policyholder behavior may impact profitability.

Term Life: Provides protection for a specified period of time. It pays a benefit only if the insured's death occurs during the coverage period. It can be considered a pure protection product and a consumer's entry-level life insurance product. Term periods typically range from one year to 30 years, although there are annually renewable policies, which are designed for longer durations. Term life, which is a highly competitive product, is marketed through many traditional distribution channels, as well as through financial institutions, banks and various direct distribution channels including the internet. More recent products offer long-term premium guarantees, where the premium is guaranteed to be the same for a given period of years. Return of premium (ROP) term products have also become popular of late, offering policyowners a refund of all premiums paid if the insured is still alive at the end of the term period. Concerns to insurers include high lapse rates, compressed margins and high reserve requirements.

Group Life: Generally in the form of term life, group life is marketed to employers or association groups. The cost also may be shared by the participant and the master policyholder, usually the employee and employer, respectively. Typically, an initial benefit level may be paid by the employer, and in some cases, employees may elect to pay for additional coverage. Like with term life, competition is intense.

Annuity Products

Insurance companies provide annuities, which at their most basic are contracts that ensure an income stream. A payment or series of payments is made to an insurance company, and in return, the insurer agrees to pay an income for a specified time period. Annuities can take many forms but have a couple of basic properties: an immediate or deferred payout with fixed (guaranteed) or variable returns. Consequently, different annuity types can resemble certificates of deposit, pensions or even investment portfolios.

Challenges to the Annuity Industry

Life insurance companies must minimize the risk of disintermediation. This happens when deferred annuity holders seeking higher-yielding alternatives withdraw funds prematurely (often during periods of increasing interest rates), and force companies to pay these surrenders by liquidating investments that may be in an unrealized loss position. Insurers can mitigate this risk by matching the duration of its interest-sensitive liability portfolio with the duration of its asset portfolio, and by selling a diversified portfolio of products. Insurers also mitigate risk by designing deferred annuities with market-value adjustments on surrender values.

Immediate Annuities: These annuities are designed to guarantee owners a pre-determined income stream on a monthly, quarterly, semiannual or annual basis in exchange for a lump sum. Options are limited from the annuity holder's perspective, so profits are generally less volatile in the short term. However, the long-term nature of these products exposes the insurer to reinvestment risk and longevity risk.

Group Annuities: These differ slightly from individual annuities in that the payout is dependent upon the life expectancy of all the members of the group rather than on the individual. Many company retirement plans, such as 401(k) plans, are annuities that will pay a regular income to the retiree. Tax-deferred annuity plans—403(b) and 457 plans—also are used widely by public-sector and nonprofit workers.

Deferred Annuities: A type of long-term savings product that allows assets to grow tax-deferred until annuitization. This product category includes:

Traditional Fixed Annuities: These products guarantee a minimum rate of interest during the time the account is growing, and typically guarantee a minimum benefit upon annuitization.

For the issuer, fixed annuities are subject to significant asset/liability mismatch risks, as described above. Also, when interest rates fall, spread earnings—or the difference between the yield on investments and credited rates—can decrease, and asset cash flows must be reinvested at lower rates.

Fixed-Indexed Annuities: These products are credited with a return that is based on changes in an equity index. The insurance company typically guarantees a minimum return. Payouts may be periodic or in a lump sum. The potential for gains is an attractive feature during favorable market conditions; however, gains may not be as favorable as those available from variable annuities or straight equity investments. Sales of these products may decline if equity markets go through a prolonged downturn or a prolonged upturn.

Variable Annuities: The participant is given a range of investment options, typically mutual funds, from which to choose. The rate of return on the purchase payment, and the amount of the periodic payments, will vary depending on the performance of the selected investments and the level of expense charges in the product.

Variable annuity sales tend to slump during unfavorable equity market conditions. In addition, the primary sources of revenue for these products are account-value-based fees, which also decline when market conditions deteriorate. Relatively thin margins, increasing product complexity (e.g., guaranteed living benefits) and volatile capital requirements put variable annuities at the riskier end of the product continuum, from the standpoint of the issuing insurer.

Because variable annuities allow for investments in equity and fixed-income securities, they are regulated by the U.S. Securities and Exchange Commission. Fixed annuities and fixed-indexed annuities are not securities, and as such, are not regulated by the SEC.

Accident & Health Products

Credit Accident & Health: This insurance covers a borrower for accidental injury, disability and related health expenses. It is designed specifically to make monthly payments until the insured can recover and resume earning income. If an individual is totally disabled for the life of the loan, the policy would pay the remaining balance, in most cases, but only one month at a time.

Group Accident & Health: These plans are designed for a natural group, such as employees of a single employer, or union members, and their dependents. Insurance is provided under a single policy, with individual certificates issued to each participant.

Other Accident & Health: Products that fall into this category could be policies for individuals that cover major medical, disability insurance, long-term care, dental, dread disease or auxiliary coverages such as Medicare supplement.

Life Coverage Comes Full Circle

A pioneer in the life settlement industry says it's time for this sector to educate consumers about the value of their life insurance policies.

From its beginning in Cleveland in 1989 when a life insurance policy was sold to pay for a dying person's medication to today where healthy consumers sell their policies for cash, Scott Page, president and CEO of the Lifeline Program, has witnessed the evolution of the life settlement industry.

You did one of the very first life settlement transactions. Can you tell us about that?

It was interesting. It was in 1989. A very dear friend of mine was trying to decide whether they could buy medications or pay their life insurance premium bill. I thought, "Wait a minute. I know you're going to die." He knew he was going to die. I felt if I could find someone to help financially it could help relieve some pressure for him and preserve the life insurance policy.

I started talking to friends. One of my dear friends and business partners at the time wrote a letter to *The Cleveland Plain Dealer*. We were in Cleveland, Ohio. On a Sunday, an opinion editorial ran. On Monday, we received a phone call from someone who said, "How can I help?" We structured the transaction. This was before the word "life settlement" existed, before the word "viatical settlement" existed. We simply were trying to do something to help.

What was the atmosphere like at that time, in those early days of the industry?

It was very different than it was today. There was no structure. There was no regulation.

Actually, we were most successful by attending the Dallas Buyers Club, which you've probably seen that movie with Matthew McConaughey. We were there in Dallas handing out brochures to HIV and AIDS patients trying to educate them about how they can turn their life insurance policy into a resource to help them pay for the medicines they needed to survive.

How has the industry changed since those early days?

Scott Page

There has been a lot more regulation, to start with. At the time, the regulation was important because it was consumer protection. These were consumers that were vulnerable. They didn't have the resources to take care of themselves. It was critical for them to understand that if they accept funds through this transaction it might interrupt their public service funds, any means-based entitlement issues, any type of gifting programs they were getting from the state.

The regulation was very important for the consumer. Now the regulation has shifted. The majority of transactions that are taking place today are called life settlements. The rule of thumb is a viatical settlement is 24 months or less. Someone with a terminal illness, a life settlement is 24 months or more.

The life settlement industry was born out of the viatical settlement industry. The regulations now are more geared toward the protection of the investment side. The individuals selling their policy through a life settlement is an average policy of a million dollars or more.

They probably would qualify for credit or investor status. They already have some type of knowledge based on the transactions and they're in a much better position if they feel they've been wronged. They have lawyers and accountants to defend them.

What challenges are the industry facing today?

The challenge now is going back to our roots and educating consumers. We're seeing a big swing back to buying viaticals. I was somewhat torn when the association decided to remove the word viatical from the name.

It used to be the Viatical and Life Settlement Association. Viatical became this bad thing. In my opinion, it was always a good thing. It was helping people survive and live. Yes, some people were able to get access to medications who had AIDS who did viatical settlements and lived and the investors lost money.

We were one of the first to launch a consumer campaign. Betty White was our official spokesperson for 10 years. We were running into issues there, just about understanding that you can sell your policy. A lot of people would see the message and then think, "Why do I need to buy a policy? I don't have a life insurance policy."

For consumers to look at their life insurance and understand it's not a liability always. It's not something you have to write a check for. This is now an asset and it has a value. There's a very healthy industry that's eager to help them understand what that value is and pay them handsomely for it.

By Meg Green

Health Market at a Glance

Health insurers focus principally on providing health coverage and related protection products. A.M. Best's database contained annual filing information for 1,227 single health insurance companies in the United States. According to the U.S. Department of Labor, more than 476,400 people worked in the health insurance industry in 2017.

Health insurers typically have shorter investment horizons than life insurers or property/casualty insurers that focus on liability coverage. Health insurers are measured by premiums and membership in their programs, sometimes known as "covered lives."

A report by the Kaiser Family Foundation estimates that in 2017, 49% of the U.S. population was covered by employer-sponsored health insurance. Another 19% was covered by Medicaid, a state-based program for those of limited financial means. Another 14% of the population was covered by Medicare, which is designed for seniors. About 9% of the U.S. population has no insurance.

Health insurance policies pay benefits to insureds who become ill or injured. Managed care is the most common form of coverage. In managed care, insurance companies establish fee agreements with doctors and hospitals to provide health care services.

If managed care health insurance is provided through employment, the employer pays the managed care plan a set amount of money in advance for all health care costs. The employee may have to contribute a portion of the premium to the employer via a payroll deduction. The employee then pays a flat amount for the services as either a copayment or a percentage of the cost of services provided.

In most managed care plans, doctors or hospitals are chosen from a network of providers. Some managed care plans allow for visits to doctors outside the network, at a greater cost to the employee.

Some of the largest carriers of health insurance are Blue Cross Blue Shield plans and publicly traded companies. Blue Cross Blue Shield companies operate independently as part of an association. Blue Cross companies originally focused on hospitalization coverage. Blue Shield companies originally focused on coverage for doctor visits. The two associations have since merged and now provide health insurance coverage options for employer groups and individuals.

Major Types of Health Plans Include:

HMO (Health Maintenance Organization): Employees select a primary care physician, who oversees all aspects of the employees' medical care and provides referrals to see specialists. Most services received from doctors or hospitals out of the plan's network are not covered.

PPO (Preferred Provider Organization): A network of doctors, hospitals and other health care providers make up the organization, but the PPO also allows an employee to go to specialists, out-of-network doctors or hospitals without needing prior authorization from a primary care physician. However, more of the costs to receive care outside the network are shouldered by the employee.

POS (Point of Service): The employee must designate a primary care physician but retains the option to receive services from doctors without a referral or go outside the network for care and shoulder much of the cost.

Fee-for-service health plans, or indemnity plans, were once the traditional route for coverage. There is no network of pre-approved providers, so an employee can choose to visit any doctor or hospital. These plans cost the most and have dwindled sharply in the past 30 years.

Some employers offer plans that combine a pretax savings account with a high-deductible health plan (HDHP) to establish a health savings account (HSA). The HSA pays for qualified and routine health care expenses with tax-free money until the deductible is met; then the insurance coverage takes over. The funds in the HSA also can be used for expenses the HDHP doesn't cover, and HSA balances carry forward to future years.

Consolidated membership and revenue growth for group health insurance has been limited, since employers have reduced head count as companies look to manage expenses.

In addition, the price of health coverage has become a focal point when employers look to provide coverage for their employees. Many employers have implemented benefit modifications to lower the impact of premium rate increases at renewal.

Products and Terms

Health products come in a wide variety of forms and address basic health needs, ranging from medical care to specialized forms of illness and accident coverage. Health products include:

Indemnity Health Plans: These may be offered on an individual or group basis. Indemnity plans allow members to choose their own doctor or hospital. The carrier then pays a fixed portion of total charges. Indemnity plans are often known as "fee-for-service" plans.

High-Deductible Health Plans: These may feature low premiums and an integrated deductible for both medical and pharmacy costs. Some plans combine a health plan with a Health Savings Account.

Health Savings Accounts: Participants may contribute pretax money to be used for qualified medical expenses. HSAs, which are portable, must be linked to a high-deductible health insurance policy.

Health Reimbursement Arrangements: HRAs are available to high-deductible health plan owners who are not qualified for health savings accounts.

Dental Plans: Traditional dental plans may help cover preventive, basic and major services.

Dental Preferred Provider Organizations: These offer discounts to members who use in-network dental providers.

Vision Plans: Vision care plans may cover regular eye exams, treatment for conditions and assistance with corrective lenses.

Pharmacy: Plans may cover part or all of prescription drug costs.

Flexible Spending Account (FSA): A program where employees may contribute pre-tax money to be used for medical expenses, including copays, coinsurance, and any non-covered services or over the counter medication.

Medicare Advantage: This provides Medicare-eligible retirees the benefits of Medicare, plus additional features and benefits such as wellness program and case management services. Retirees who select Medicare Advantage agree to use in-network doctors and hospitals or face much higher out-of pocket costs.

Common Health Insurance Terms Include:

Coinsurance: For health insurance, it is a percentage of each claim above the deductible paid by the policyholder. For a 20% health insurance coinsurance clause, the policyholder pays for the deductible plus 20% of covered losses. After paying 80% of losses up to a specified ceiling, the insurer starts paying 100% of losses.

Copayment: A predetermined, flat fee an individual pays for health care services, in addition to what insurance covers. For example, some HMOs require a $20 copayment for each office visit, regardless of the type or level of services provided during the visit. Copayments are not usually specified by percentages.

Disease Management: A system of coordinated health care interventions and communications for patients with certain medical conditions.

Developing Issues

According to A.M. Best's annual *Review & Preview* report on the U.S. health insurance sector, insurers are adapting to a business landscape shaped as much by social and regulatory issues as it is by competition.

Health insurers are looking at initiatives to better control the cost of care, which includes disease management programs and improved coordination of care. As a result, there has been increased collaboration with providers, and that can benefit all parties, including the patient. Health insurers are able to give providers data that can be used to monitor patients and help ensure that proper treatment is obtained. This is particularly important for higher risk individuals, as lack of appropriate treatment could lead to deterioration of the medical condition and potential hospitalization.

Changing the Customer Experience

In response to the continuing evolution of the health insurance marketplace, health insurers are paying careful attention to the customer experience. This change in focus is being driven by several factors, including a shift in the health insurance purchase from the employer to the individual consumer, as well as the presence of millennials, who have different needs. Furthermore, with the implementation of the Patient Protection and Affordable Care Act (PPACA) and exchange products, some purchasers are viewing health insurance as a commoditized product where price can be the determining factor. As a result, carriers are trying to find a way to differentiate themselves and meet the needs of different groups of customers.

Millennials are a big challenge because they approach health care and health insurance in an entirely different way than their parents or grandparents. Often called "young invincibles," this age group does not see the value in health insurance, mostly due to being young and healthy. Additionally, under a provision of the PPACA, they are allowed to remain on their parents' policies until age 26, so they do not need to be active participants in the selection of their health insurance until they age out. These younger generation purchasers are interested in plans that give them choice, flexibility and ease of use, with an emphasis on quality and value. Millennials look for convenience in a health plan and in access to health care. These individuals prefer to access information through an app, ask customer service representatives questions through an online chat, locate retail clinics in their network via the internet and utilize telemedicine. Additionally, millennials are highly likely to look at customer comments or reviews on the web, so public perception of an insurer is important.

In addition, many carriers are adopting a model in which the member is at the center of all operating activities and business strategies, with special attention to satisfaction metrics. High levels of customer satisfaction can result in better retention rates and medical compliance. Plans are collecting data, including customer feedback, to perform analysis geared toward measuring how well they are reaching customer expectations. Some carriers are also analyzing customer service inquiries to understand the primary reason for these contacts, to better address member concerns and to improve operations so customer service is increased and the need for inquiries is decreased.

Health carriers are creating additional avenues for consumer engagement and expanding member access to information. The mindset is for health plans to make available consumer-desired access points, whether it is communication in a specific language, in-person interaction or use of different media such as phone, web, email and mobile technology. Furthermore, consumers want plans that are easy to purchase, understand and use. Plan designs that include deductibles, co-insurance, different in- and out-of-network coverage, as well as out-of-pocket maximums, can be confusing.

Insurers are utilizing data analytics to personalize member communications regarding their health plan and care. They are also making available transparency tools, including cost estimators and provider quality data. In the internet age, consumers are used to being able to do cost comparison and look up reviews or ratings to be able to make informed decisions when they make purchases.

Beyond Good Intentions:
Behavioral Science Makes Its Mark

Josh Wright of Ideas42 posed an unusual question to his audience at recent conference: Are humans more like Mr. Spock or Homer Simpson?

The answer, the behavioral economist said, is that we fall somewhere between the logical Star Trek science officer and the emotional cartoon dad. We are a rational yet quirky species, biased toward the present, bad at recognizing probabilities and overconfident in our odds.

"That makes insurance hard for people," Wright said.

Wright is an executive director at Ideas42, a design and research lab that uses behavioral economics to address social problems. He speaks frequently on the role of behavioral economics in financial services and gave a presentation on the topic at InsureTech Connect in Las Vegas.

Looking at the insurance industry, what are the main problems you're trying to solve?

There's a huge scope in the insurance industry. I would start on the consumer side. There are opportunities around honesty and making claims, for example. It's not that people are dishonest or are trying to deeply cheat. But if there's an opportunity to fudge a little bit, they think other people are doing that and that they are entitled to do it in some way also. So there's a lot of opportunity around honesty of claims.

Practically speaking, how can insurers make policyholders more honest about claims?

There was insight from [Harvard Business School Professor] Max Bazerman, where if you ask people to sign their name on a form, such as a claims form, before they fill in their information, versus having them sign after, they're more likely to be honest if they've signed first.

Why is that?

They don't know with absolute certainty. Basically the hypothesis is that you're asking them to say they're going to enter this information on this form truthfully, so they're primed for honesty.

If they enter all the information, and after the fact you ask them to attest to it being valid, it may cause them to have to go

Josh Wright

back and change it or admit to themselves that they lied. So the theory is that you're priming them to tell the truth by having them sign first.

There are going to be some people who are very intentionally trying to cheat in a big way, whatever the process is, but most people are generally trying to be honest, but they fudge a little bit.

How can insurers use behavioral science to increase customer satisfaction?

You might think people's experiences with a product or procedure or service are based on some amalgamation of all the time they've interacted with that service, meaning you buy the insurance in the beginning, you make a claim, your claim gets paid.

If you're rating the experience overall, you'd think all those things might be similarly factored in. But, actually, what behavioral science shows us is that the end effect is the most important. If you make an experience less painful and more enjoyable at the end, there's a recency bias that makes their overall perspective on the entire experience happier.

There have been a number of studies on that. At the InsureTech conference I cited one around colonoscopies. With the colonoscopy test, they randomized people. In one case, they did the normal procedure. In the other case, at the end of the procedure they had a pause moment for about 30 seconds where they didn't do anything, which means there was almost no pain for people at the time. Not only did those people report lower levels of pain, but they also were more likely to

come back and get a colonoscopy five years later, because they had this end effect versus the peak effect in terms of their experience of pain or happiness.

Insurance companies might think about how important it is at the end of the whole experience to leave people feeling quite happy.

Can you give me an example of how they could do that?

For example, when they're paying out a claim or fixing a person's car, they could really go above and beyond to make sure the customer has a really good experience and feels their needs were met. Were they happy with their experience? Did the problem fully get resolved for them? Focusing on the end part of the process and the interaction with the customer is a huge opportunity.

Most insurance companies, even the ones that are more focused on customer satisfaction, think they need to make the whole process better for people. Which is true, you do need to improve the whole process. But if you're thinking about where your return on investment is, you should go to the end of the process and make it as pleasurable as possible.

In the auto insurance segment, plug-in devices are being used as behavior-modification tools. Are they an effective way to create desired behaviors?

I actually think something like [Progressive's] Snapshot, from a behavioral perspective, is underutilized.

BEST

There could be more opportunities to give people real-time feedback about their driving. What if you knew you didn't want to drive aggressively, and you recorded in your own voice, "Hey Josh, remember to be a calm driver"? It could play a message from your past self telling your current self that you're driving in a hazardous way.

From a behavioral science standpoint, is hearing that message in your own voice more effective than a computerized voice?

The most powerful thing might be if I recorded my 12-year-old daughter telling me she wanted me to drive safely. That's more powerful than a computer telling you the same thing.

Part of having the message in your own voice is that it reminds you that this is something you yourself want to do. It's not someone else telling you to do it. It's the thing you said you wanted to do. The loved one saying it is even more powerful because it's a personalization of their love for you.

In behavioral economics, we think about how our preferences change over time. We talk about past self, current self and future self. Your preferences are not the same over time. This is a great example. If you ask me whether I want to be a better driver, have a bigger discount, use less fuel by not accelerating, right now, as I sit in my office, I'd say "Sure."

Then I go out driving, and maybe I'm rushing to get somewhere and someone cuts me off. That calm, sitting-at-my-desk self goes away and Mario Andretti comes out.

If you ask me after I've gotten home if I wish I drove less aggressively, the sitting-at-my-desk self again says, "Sure."

So there is some evidence that you can use technology to send your different selves different messages. If I'm sitting at my desk, I want my future self to know that when I drive, I should do certain things. Then, in that moment, my past self is delivering a message.

We've talked quite a bit about using behavioral science to interact with the end consumer. How can insurance companies use it within their internal operations?

In underwriting processes and uses of data, behavioral economics can be quite useful. This is the other side of the coin. You have people who are doing underwriting and handling claims. We should realize those people have their own biases and their mind might not always work in the way they'd ideally like it to work. There are things in the underwriting processes where you'd want to account for human biases. Very closely connected to that is the use of data. Big data has already hit insurance, but it's hard to get people to use it. Underwriters and claims adjusters look at data, but they're still making the decisions on their own. We've done some work around how to present that information in a way that doesn't make people feel like the machine is taking over and taking their job.

By Kate Smith

Overview of Reinsurance

Broadly put, reinsurance is insurance for insurers.

Insurance companies face many risks in their daily operations, including:

Asset risks, or the changing nature of investment values.

Credit risk, or the obligations owed by customers and/or debtors.

Liability risk, or potential losses due to inadequate pricing or reserving, or from catastrophes and other events.

Estimate for Total Dedicated Reinsurance Capacity

Source: A.M. Best data and research, working in conjunction with Guy Carpenter

Reinsurance is a transaction that indemnifies the primary insurer against those potential losses. The primary insurer, or ceding company, transfers a portion of risk to the reinsurer. How much risk and what conditions trigger the reinsurance are specified in the treaties. Generally, the primary carrier retains a fair amount of the risk.

Reinsurance allows insurers to increase the maximum amount they can insure. However, most reinsurance contracts do not absolve the ceding insurer's responsibility to pay the insurance claims should the reinsurer fail. The first reinsurance companies were born out of a major fire in 1842 that burned a large section of Hamburg, Germany, and killed at least 50 people. The conflagration exposed the inability of insurers to cope with such a catastrophe, and the insurers recognized the need to distribute risk portfolios among several carriers.

For a basic reinsurance scenario, take an office building worth $20 million. A primary carrier may accept the risk of loss and then turn to a reinsurer, agreeing to cover the first $10 million and ceding the rest. If losses at the building then were to exceed the primary layer of $10 million, say $14 million, the reinsurer would be called upon to cover the remaining $4 million.

In a case like this, the arrangement is said to be a nonproportional agreement, also known as an excess of loss agreement. In proportional agreements, the primary insurer and reinsurer share the liability risk proportionately. In the case of a quota share agreement, the primary insurer and reinsurer split the premiums and losses on a fixed percentage basis.

The two basic types of reinsurance arrangements are treaty and facultative. Treaty reinsurance contractually binds the insurer and reinsurer together, with respect to certain specified business. The treaty requires the insurer to cede all the risks specified by the agreement with the reinsurer, and the reinsurer must assume those specified risks. This means that the reinsurer automatically takes the risk for all policies that are covered by the treaty, and not just one particular policy.

Facultative reinsurance, on the other hand, is done more on a case-by-case basis. The reinsurance is issued after an individual analysis of the situation and by deciding coverage case by case. The reinsurer can determine if it wants some or all of the risk associated with that particular policy. This arrangement usually takes place when the risks are so unusual or so large that they aren't covered in the insurance company's standard reinsurance treaties.

Reinsurers also can purchase reinsurance to cover their own risk exposure or to increase their capacity. This process is called a retrocession. *how does this work?*

Developing Issues in Reinsurance

A.M. Best's 2017 *Review & Preview* report on the global reinsurance industry identifies several issues shaping the reinsurance industry, including weaker financial performance, the impact of merger activity and pressure from investors in alternative capital.

A.M. Best continues to hold its outlook for the reinsurance sector at negative, citing the significant ongoing market challenges that will hinder the potential for positive rating actions over time and may eventually translate into negative rating pressures. The market is in the later stages of a soft market.

Risk-adjusted returns are strained, as compression continues bearing down on underwriting margins, and investment yields offer little help. The market headwinds at this point present significant longer-term challenges that industry players need to work through. We've said that the companies that are not proactive will not determine their own destiny. M&A

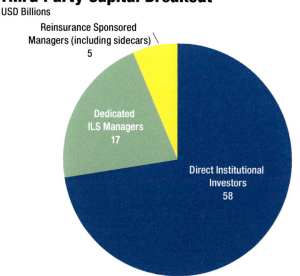

Third Party Capital Breakout
USD Billions

Reinsurance Sponsored Managers (including sidecars) — 5
Dedicated ILS Managers — 17
Direct Institutional Investors — 58

Source: A.M. Best data and research, working in conjunction with Guy Carpenter

will remain a part of the landscape over the next few years, but M&A is not a cure and has its own potential dangers.

Declining rates, broader terms and conditions, an unsustainable flow of net favorable loss reserve development, low investment yields and continued pressures from convergence capital are all negative factors that will adversely affect risk adjusted returns over the longer term. Adding to the uncertainty is the potential fallout from Brexit or what type of changes, if any, will come to pass with regard to U.S. taxes. There are some pockets of opportunity with cyber insurance and mortgage reinsurance, but these do not come without risk and by themselves aren't enough to buoy the market in a meaningful way.

Reinsurers have been responding in other ways, by lowering their net probable maximum loss (PML) for peak zones, embracing new opportunities and geographies, producing fee income and subtly migrating into asset classes that will produce some increased investment yield. Nevertheless, even with benign catastrophe conditions and stable financial markets, the overall market will produce a return on equity only in the mid to high single digits. The reality of the current situation is that even a normal catastrophe year will expose the true ramifications of current market conditions; an above average catastrophe year may be downright ugly.

For the most part, rated balance sheets are well capitalized and capable of enduring a fair amount of stress. However, this strength may be eroded for some carriers as earnings come under increased pressure, favorable reserve development fades, and the ability to earn back losses following events is hindered by the immediate inflow of capital and competition from both traditional and non-traditional sources.

Our view of strong companies remains the same as it has for a number of years. Companies with diverse business portfolios, advanced distribution capabilities, and broad geographic scope are better positioned to withstand the pressures in this type of operating environment and will be better able to target profitable opportunities as they arise.

The Growth of Alternative Capital

Alternative sources of capacity began to enter the market attracted by the increased reliability of risk models, diversification benefits and potential returns to investors. The low-yield environment that has been in place since the 2008 financial crisis has made these types of investments all the more compelling for investors.

The proliferation of efficient structures (sidecars) and insurance-linked securities (ILS) allowed for a shorter time horizon (one to three years), in addition to a relatively quick entry into and exit from the reinsurance market. Originally, reinsurers such as Hannover Re, Swiss Re and Munich Re were the leaders in the utilization of alternative capacity, largely provided by pension plans, sovereign wealth funds and hedge funds. The majority of this capacity was and has been deployed in the form of ILS and collateralized pools or temporary sidecars.

More recently, investors and users of this capacity are bypassing the traditional reinsurer and transferring risk directly to the capital markets. Lower interest rates have led to an increased inflow of alternative capital as investors look for uncorrelated ways to improve returns. This phenomenon has given rise to collateralized funds, unrated sidecars, more flexible forms of ILS and the birth of "Hedge Fund Re," looking to optimize investment returns offshore while building a base of long-term assets under management.

According to Guy Carpenter and A.M. Best data and research, today's convergence capacity totals $85 billion, supplementing the $345 billion available via traditional

Top 25 World's Largest Reinsurance Groups
(Ranked by Unaffiliated Gross Premiums Written in 2016)
(USD Millions)[1]

| 2017 Ranking | Company Name | Reinsurance Premiums Written | | | | Total Shareholders' Funds[2] | <----------Ratios[3]----------> | | |
| | | Life & Non-Life | | Non-Life Only | | | | | |
		Gross	Net	Gross	Net		Loss	Expense	Combined
1	Swiss Re Ltd.	$35,622	$33,570	$21,878	$21,430	$35,716	61.3%	33.6%	94.8%
2	Munich Reinsurance Company	$33,154	$31,891	$18,784	$17,931	$33,493	63.3%	32.4%	95.8%
3	Hannover Rück S.E.[4]	$17,232	$15,192	$9,699	$8,414	$10,264	66.8%	27.2%	94.0%
4	SCOR S.E.	$14,569	$13,238	$5,942	$5,323	$7,055	59.5%	33.6%	93.1%
5	Berkshire Hathaway Inc.[5]	$12,709	$12,709	$8,037	$8,037	$286,359	N/A	N/A	89.4%
6	Lloyd's[6][7]	$11,576	$8,694	$11,576	$8,694	$34,101	53.2%	39.2%	92.3%
7	Reinsurance Group of America Inc.	$10,107	$9,249	N/A	N/A	$7,093	N/A	N/A	N/A
8	China Reinsurance (Group) Corporation	$7,857	$7,517	$3,342	$3,262	$10,384	64.4%	37.5%	101.9%
9	Great West Lifeco	$6,195	$6,112	N/A	N/A	$13,857	N/A	N/A	N/A
10	Korean Reinsurance Company	$5,554	$3,903	$4,880	$3,312	$1,755	81.7%	17.6%	99.2%
11	PartnerRe Ltd.	$5,357	$4,954	$4,189	$3,837	$6,688	60.2%	33.4%	93.6%
12	General Insurance Corporation of India[8]	$5,210	$4,678	$5,153	$4,626	$7,681	79.8%	21.4%	101.1%
13	Transatlantic Holdings, Inc.	$4,330	$3,969	$4,330	$3,969	$5,203	59.5%	33.8%	93.2%
14	Everest Re Group Ltd.[9]	$4,247	$3,885	$4,247	$3,885	$8,075	50.1%	27.5%	77.6%
15	XL Group Ltd.	$4,240	$3,527	$3,975	$3,515	$12,961	56.3%	32.1%	88.4%
16	MS&AD Insurance Group Holdings, Inc. [8][10][17]	$3,192	N/A	$3,192	N/A	$24,583	N/A	N/A	N/A
17	MAPFRE RE, Compania de Reaseguros S.A. [11]	$2,426	$2,180	$1,813	$1,584	$1,348	68.3%	23.6%	91.9%
18	RenaissanceRe Holdings Ltd.	$2,375	$1,535	$2,375	$1,535	$4,867	37.8%	34.7%	72.5%
19	R+V Versicherung AG[12]	$2,348	$2,305	$2,348	$2,305	$2,265	73.8%	25.3%	99.1%
20	The Toa Reinsurance Company, Limited [8][10]	$2,251	$1,970	$2,251	$1,970	$1,725	67.7%	26.0%	93.7%
21	Axis Capital Holdings Limited	$2,250	$1,946	$2,250	$1,946	$6,272	55.1%	32.8%	87.8%
22	Arch Capital Group Ltd.[13]	$2,029	$1,568	$2,029	$1,568	$9,106	52.3%	33.5%	85.8%
23	Assicurazioni Generali SpA	$1,936	$1,936	$791	$791	$27,047	56.0%	23.3%	79.3%
24	QBE Insurance Group Limited	$1,698	$1,390	$1,698	$1,390	$10,334	55.1%	32.7%	87.8%
25	Endurance Specialty Holdings, Ltd.	$1,632	$1,314	$1,632	$1,314	$5,142	47.0%	30.9%	77.9%

[1] All non-USD currencies converted to USD using foreign exchange rate at company's fiscal year-end.
[2] As reported on balance sheet.
[3] Non-Life only.
[4] Net premium written data not reported, net premium earned substituted.
[5] Loss and expense ratio detail not available on a GAAP basis.
[6] Lloyd's premiums are reinsurance only. Premiums for certain groups within the rankings also may include Lloyd's Syndicate premiums when applicable.
[7] Total shareholders' funds includes Lloyd's members' assets and Lloyd's central reserves.

[8] Fiscal year-end March 31, 2017.
[9] Based on Everest Re Group Ltd. consolidated financial statements and includes cessions to Mt. Logan Re Ltd.
[10] Net asset value used for total shareholders' funds.
[11] Premium data excludes intergroup reinsurance.
[12] Ratios are as reported and calculated on a gross basis.
[13] Based on Arch Capital Group Ltd. consolidated financial statements and includes Watford Re segment.

Source: A.M. Best data and research

capacity in the global reinsurance market in the first half of 2017. Competition for U.S. property catastrophe business has been fierce since third-party capital exploded into the market (starting in earnest around 2006). The pressure has since rippled to other classes and geographies as capacity is reallocated.

Alternative Risk Transfer and Risk Financing

The blurring of boundaries between insurance and capital markets is most evident in structured finance, part of an area that is broadly known as alternative risk transfer (ART).

The highest-profile members of the ART community are captives—insurance or reinsurance companies owned by their insured clients and located in jurisdictions, or domiciles, that may be tax friendly or may have reduced capital and reserve requirements. Captives typically are formed by one or more noninsurance companies when traditional market coverage is more limited, or when the parent companies wish to have more direct control of their own risks.

Structured finance is a complex process of transferring risk, often with the purpose of raising capital. Much of the activity revolves around risk securitization, whereby the involved assets are not used as collateral as is typically found in a loan scenario. Instead, funds from investors are advanced to the originator based on the history of those assets, indicating a cash flow into the originator's business. The assets are then transferred by the originator to a separate legal entity—a special purpose vehicle (SPV)—that in turn issues securities to the investors. Interest and principal paid on those securities are financed by the cash flow.

Insurance-Linked Securities And Structured Transactions

Capital markets participants, reinsurers, brokers and insurers continue to collaborate in various combinations to create new risk-based offerings, including:

Natural Catastrophe Bonds: An alternative to reinsurance, these securities are used by insurers to protect themselves from natural catastrophes. Typically, they pay higher yields because investors could lose their entire stake in the event of a disaster. If the catastrophe happens, the funds go to the insurer to cover claims.

Sidecars: Separate, limited purpose companies, generally formed and funded by investors (usually hedge funds) that work in tandem with insurance companies. The reinsurance sidecar purchases certain insurance policies from an insurer and shares in the profits and risks. It is a way for an insurer to share risk. If the policies have low claim rates while in possession of the sidecar, the investors will make higher returns.

Surplus Notes and Insurance Trust-Preferred CDOs: Surplus notes and trust-preferred CDOs (collateralized debt obligations) provide another funding source for small and midsize insurance companies that find it costly to issue capital on their own. These companies can access the capital markets through the use of the surplus notes/insurance trust-preferred pools. Securities in these pools are issued by a stand-alone SPV and sold to investors. The proceeds of the notes are used to purchase the transaction's collateral, which consists of surplus notes and insurance trust-preferred securities.

Embedded Value (Closed Block) Securitizations: An insurer can close a block of policies to new business and receive immediate cash from investors in exchange for some or all of the future earnings on that block of business. The pledged assets remain with the insurer and are potentially available in the event of an insolvency.

Securitization of Structured Settlements: A structured settlement is an annuity used for settling personal injury, product liability, medical malpractice and wrongful death cases. The defendant (typically, a liability insurer) discharges its obligation by purchasing an annuity from a highly rated life insurance company. Securitization of annuity cash flows is achieved through the use of a bankruptcy-remote SPV. The issuer of the securities, the SPV, raises funds from investors that are used to purchase annuity cash flows from the annuitants. The cash flows received by the issuer are used primarily to service the principal and interest payments due the investors.

Mortality Catastrophe Bonds: Investors in these bonds lose money only if a level of deaths linked to a catastrophic event exceeds a certain threshold. The event's trigger is extreme (for example, a pandemic). These are a derivative of natural cat bonds.

Life Settlement Securitizations: A life settlement contract is a way for a policyholder to liquidate a life insurance policy. A portfolio of these contracts may be securitized to provide a source of capital. However, certain variables, such as regulatory issues and the uncertainties

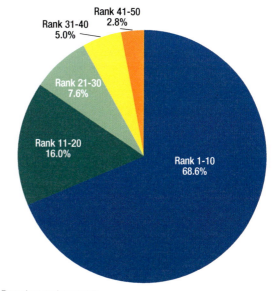

Life and Non-Life Reinsurance Gross Premiums Written Distribution by Ranking

Rank 41-50 2.8%
Rank 31-40 5.0%
Rank 21-30 7.6%
Rank 11-20 16.0%
Rank 1-10 68.6%

Source: A.M. Best data and research

associated with predicting life expectancies, can create obstacles that may slow their path to the marketplace.

Securitization of Reinsurance Recoverables: Insurance and reinsurance companies have been finding alternative ways to reduce their exposure to uncollectible recoverables and reduce the concentration risk associated with ceded exposures. One approach is the securitization of reinsurance recoverables, which involves a structured debt instrument that transfers risk associated with the risk of uncollectible reinsurance to the capital markets. This risk transfer may also be accomplished through the use of collateralized debt obligation (CDO) technology.

Insurers Leverage the New Economy

The sharing economy encompasses five sectors, according to PwC. It includes collaborative finance, peer-to-peer accommodation, peer-to-peer transportation, on-demand household services and on-demand professional services. Think Uber, Airbnb, Lending Club, TaskRabbit and Sittercity—some of the public faces of this socioeconomic phenomenon. The sharing economy is disrupting entire industries. Insurance is not immune.

"The fundamental premise of what we're seeing is a dramatic difference in understanding the nature of risk, people's behaviors and asset utilization. That is what is disrupting this industry," said Michael Costonis, senior managing director in Accenture's financial services practice. "It's not just people and cars. It's how goods move around. It's how buildings get built. We can monitor these things in real time. It completely changes the way an insurance company can understand what's happening in order to provide products and services against that."

The new economy is forcing insurers to rethink how they structure, underwrite, price and distribute products. The on-demand world expects on-demand insurance, with instantaneous underwriting and flexible products that are digitally distributed.

"It creates a brand-new opportunity for companies that can be both innovative and agile around product development to capture the market opportunity," Costonis said.

Experts say insurers are still trying to figure out what, exactly, those products look like and how to meet the needs of participants in this new economy.

"Over the last year I have seen more carriers taking a much more active position in trying to understand where the sharing economy is going and how they need to adapt to this," said Francois Ramette, partner in the PwC Advisory insurance practice. "I wouldn't have made that statement two years ago."

Embracing Change
The sharing economy was met with resistance initially. Home sharing and ride sharing blur the lines between personal and commercial use. They fall squarely between insurance lines, and insurers had no solution for their hybrid nature.

"One of the biggest challenges is that the gig economy promotes using personal assets, such as your home or car, for

Arlene Kern

commercial use," said Arlene Kern, strategic innovation leader at Munich Reinsurance America. "Traditional personal lines insurance products are not designed to contemplate those types of risks."

The early response was to not cover them. "At the beginning, the personal lines industry was caught off guard that this was taking place," said Randy Nornes, executive vice president of Aon Risk Solutions. "There was commercial activity, but when did it begin and when did it end? So at first there was a pretty hard pushback from the personal lines industry to say they weren't going to cover it.

"But you've seen that change pretty dramatically. The insurance industry has generally responded pretty well once the landscape was laid out and they knew what problem they were trying to solve for."

Kern agrees the mindset has changed. "We're seeing a growing shift from finding reasons that it can't work toward finding ways to make it work," she said.

The first solution has been to add gap coverage to existing policies. But that is a baby step. To stay competitive in this growing market, traditional insurers need to get a bit more creative.

The incumbents are facing challengers. In recent years, startups such as Trov, Slice and Metromile have popped up with innovative coverages designed specifically for this new economy. They offer on-demand insurance, bought and bound with the swipe of a finger.

"There's a whole trend around insurance on-demand," Ramette said. "You can start and stop your insurance policy when you need it. The technology that enables those types of products will definitely enable the development of the sharing economy."

It also will push traditional insurers to reimagine how the industry can work.

"The proliferation of on-demand products that mirror the gig economy may cause the insurance industry to rip up the playbook as it seeks new ways to respond to its customers' changing needs," Kern said.

Identifying those needs is the first step and one that some are still working on.

"The big shift from the insurer standpoint and the regulator standpoint is in understanding what's actually happening so they can tailor products to meet the needs," Nornes said. "There's no mystery to it once you understand what's out there and how it's working. But a lot of people in the early stages, and maybe even still today, had a set of assumptions about what is going on. So we aren't on point with what the regulation needs to look like and what the insurance products need to look like."

Insurers also need to reevaluate their own technology platforms, many of which were not designed for the flexibility required to serve participants of the new economy.

By Kate Smith

Insurance Stands
The Traditional Business Cycle on Its Head

Most industries work as follows:

- Build product.
- Incur costs.
- Price product.
- Sell product.
- Generate revenue.

But insurance works largely in reverse:

- Build product.
- Price product.
- Sell product.
- Generate revenue.
- Incur costs.

The significance of this reversed revenue/cost cycle is that the product is priced and sold based on an estimate of future costs to be incurred. These estimates can be wrong for any number of reasons, including catastrophes, claim cost inflation, changes in legal climate, newly identified exposures not known at the time the insurance policy was sold, social changes, investment market fluctuations and other factors.

This means that insurers must be very good at predicting the future and very prudent in administering their business over the long term. It directly results in what are known as underwriting cycles. It's also an important reason why the number of insurance insolvencies sometimes spikes in periods following catastrophes or market disruptions.

The insurance industry is less tangible in that the actual cost of its product isn't precisely known at the time of sale. The true cost is determined at a later point, often much later. Yet risk is taken on along with unpredictable, exogenous factors that ultimately determine profit or loss. While insurers gauge the probability of a large catastrophic event or some latent liability, these scenarios still cause a supply shock. A simplified explanation is that the insurance cycle is driven by supply and demand. If capacity is lacking, the price of risk goes up. Too much capacity and prices drift down. At some point, the downward drift is too far and balance sheets end up in need of repair, A.M. Best's annual report on the global reinsurance industry has noted.

BEST

Fiscal Fitness and A.M. Best

The Risk of Financial Impairment

The business of insurance, because of the inverted cycle in which revenues are received well before claims are incurred and must be paid (or even known), presents special concerns. There are a myriad of issues but the basic concern is assuring, to the extent reasonably possible, that insurance policy premiums and deposits received by an insurer today will be properly managed and available for payment of claims and other policy benefits (perhaps many years) in the future.

As a result, the insurance industry is subject to extensive regulation in the United States and in most other countries. In general, regulatory oversight focuses on three primary elements: (i) market soundness, including rate regulation and promoting adequate insurance availability and healthy levels of competition; (ii) market conduct, including review of market participant practices to assure proper conduct and fairness in dealings with customers; and (iii) financial soundness, including ongoing surveillance of insurance entities' financial condition and a variety of possible regulatory actions that may be taken if there are indications of financial distress.

In the United States, these financial soundness regulatory actions may consist of required company action plans, various forms and levels of regulatory supervision and licensure actions. In certain instances these actions are insufficient and the next level of action involves conservation, rehabilitation and/or insolvent liquidation. Conservation is undertaken in certain cases for the purpose of obtaining control of the entity and conserving assets while a review of the situation is conducted. Rehabilitation is undertaken when it appears that special actions are required to maintain the entity's solvency, but with these actions, solvency appears possible. Insolvent liquidation is judged necessary when it is clear that the entity's assets will not be sufficient to discharge all of the entity's obligations.

A.M. Best studies impairments carefully and produces detailed reports each year. From 2000 to 2015, in the United States there were 337 property/casualty insurer and 143 life and health insurer impairments (defined for this purpose as conservation, rehabilitation or insolvent liquidation actions taken under court order or without court involvement if regulatory actions have been taken to limit or delay claims, benefits or other payments to policyholders).

On the property/casualty side, impairments varied by line of business, with workers compensation insurers suffering the most impairments (28% of the total). Specific causes were noted for 90 of the 337 impairments, with fraud being the leading particularly identified cause, but most failures can be understood as general business failures associated with poor business strategy/execution and weak management.

On the life and health side, 70% of the impairments from 2000 to 2015 related to accident and health or health insurers, while another 16% related to small life insurers primarily focused in selling lower policy value industrial/burial or stipulated premium business. Specific causes were seen for 34 of the 143 impairments and, as with property/casualty impairments, the number-one specific cause was fraud.

State guaranty funds exist to cover unpaid claims of insolvent insurers, but these guaranty funds are generally limited in the coverage they provide to certain types of insurance and with thresholds of the amounts they can pay. There may also be considerable delays associated with payments by guaranty funds.

It therefore continues to be in the strong interest to policyholders to choose their insurance provider carefully and to monitor the provider's financial health throughout the policy period. A.M. Best has a strong role in this effort by providing interactive ratings evaluations on an ongoing basis.

The A.M. Best interactive rating process is voluntary and subjects companies to independent, oPbjective evaluations of balance sheet strength, operating performance and other critical factors. Not surprisingly, impairments have occurred much more frequently with companies choosing not to subject themselves to this rigorous process.

On the property/casualty side, 39% of the entities impaired during 2000-2015 were rated at any time by A.M. Best during the year of impairment or the three prior years. By the year of impairment, this dropped to 28% and the average A.M. Best Financial Strength Rating assigned to these entities was C+ (Marginal).

On the life and health side, 22% of the entities impaired during 2000-2015 were rated at any time by A.M. Best during the year of impairment or the three prior years. In the year of impairment, this dropped to 15% and the average A.M. Best Financial Strength Rating assigned was also C+ (Marginal).

Overview: Best's Credit Rating Evaluation

This section is from *Best's Credit Rating Methodology: Global Life and Non-Life Insurance Edition*. The primary objective of Best's Credit Ratings within the insurance segment is to provide an opinion of the rated entity's ability to meet its senior financial obligations, which for an operating insurance company are its ongoing insurance policy and contract obligations. The assignment of a Best's Credit Rating is derived from an in-depth evaluation of a company's balance sheet strength, operating performance and business profile, as compared with A.M. Best's quantitative and qualitative standards.

In determining a company's ability to meet its current and ongoing obligations, the most important area to evaluate is its balance sheet strength, since it is the foundation for financial security. Balance sheet strength measures the exposure of a company's equity or surplus to volatility based on its operating and financial practices, and can reflect its capital-generation capabilities resulting from quality of earnings. One of the primary tools used to evaluate an insurer's balance sheet strength is Best's Capital Adequacy Ratio (BCAR), which provides a quantitative measure of the risks inherent in a company's investment and insurance profile, relative to its risk-adjusted capital. A.M. Best's analysis of the balance sheet also encompasses a thorough review of various financial tests and ratios over five-year and in some cases 10-year periods.

Long-Term ICR	FSR
aaa, aa+	A++
aa, aa-	A+
a+, a	A
a-	A-
bbb+, bbb	B++
bbb-	B+
bb+, bb	B
bb-	B-
b+, b	C++
b-	C+
ccc+, ccc	C
ccc-, cc	C-
c	D

FSR = Financial Strength Rating
ICR = Issuer Credit Rating

Note: D is used for non-insurers and securities.
The rating symbols A++, A+, A, A-, B++, B+ are registered certification marks of A.M. Best Rating Services.

The assessment of balance sheet strength includes an analysis of an organization's regulatory filings at the operating insurance company, holding company and consolidated levels. To assess the financial strength and financial flexibility of a rated entity, a variety of balance sheet, income statement and cash-flow metrics are reviewed, including corporate capital structure, financial leverage, interest expense coverage, cash coverage, liquidity, capital generation, and historical sources and uses of capital.

While balance sheet strength is the foundation for financial security, it provides an assessment of capital adequacy at a point in time. A.M. Best views operating performance and business profile as leading indicators when measuring future balance sheet strength and long-term financial stability.

The term "future" is the key, since ratings are prospective and go well beyond a "static" balance sheet view. Profitability is the engine that ultimately drives capital, and looking out into the future enables the analyst to gauge a company's ability to preserve and/or generate new capital over time. In many respects, what determines the relative strength or weakness of a company's operating performance is a combination of its business profile and its ability to effectively execute its strategy.

A company exhibiting strong performance over time will generate earnings sufficient to maintain a prudent level of risk-adjusted capital and optimize stakeholder value. Strong performers are those companies whose earnings are relatively consistent and deemed to be sustainable. Companies with a stable track record and better than average earnings power may receive higher ratings and have lower risk-adjusted capital relative to their peers.

On the other hand, companies that have demonstrated weaknesses in their earnings—through either consistent losses or volatility—are more likely to struggle to maintain or improve capital in the future. For these reasons, these companies typically are rated lower than their counterparts that perform well and usually are held to higher than minimum capital guidelines to minimize the chance of being downgraded if established trends were to continue.

A.M. Best believes that risk management is the common thread that links balance sheet strength, operating performance and business profile. Risk management fundamentals can be found in the strategic decision-making process used by a company to define its business profile, and in the various financial management practices and operating elements of an insurer that dictate the sustainability

BEST'S FINANCIAL STRENGTH RATING GUIDE – (FSR)

A Best's Financial Strength Rating (FSR) is an independent opinion of an insurer's financial strength and ability to meet its ongoing insurance policy and contract obligations. An FSR is not assigned to specific insurance policies or contracts and does not address any other risk, including, but not limited to, an insurer's claims-payment policies or procedures; the ability of the insurer to dispute or deny claims payment on grounds of misrepresentation or fraud; or any specific liability contractually borne by the policy or contract holder. An FSR is not a recommendation to purchase, hold or terminate any insurance policy, contract or any other financial obligation issued by an insurer, nor does it address the suitability of any particular policy or contract for a specific purpose or purchaser. In addition, an FSR may be displayed with a rating identifier, modifier or affiliation code that denotes a unique aspect of the opinion.

Best's Financial Strength Rating (FSR) Scale

Rating Categories	Rating Symbols	Rating Notches*	Category Definitions
Superior	A+	A++	Assigned to insurance companies that have, in our opinion, a superior ability to meet their ongoing insurance obligations.
Excellent	A	A-	Assigned to insurance companies that have, in our opinion, an excellent ability to meet their ongoing insurance obligations.
Good	B+	B++	Assigned to insurance companies that have, in our opinion, a good ability to meet their ongoing insurance obligations.
Fair	B	B-	Assigned to insurance companies that have, in our opinion, a fair ability to meet their ongoing insurance obligations. Financial strength is vulnerable to adverse changes in underwriting and economic conditions.
Marginal	C+	C++	Assigned to insurance companies that have, in our opinion, a marginal ability to meet their ongoing insurance obligations. Financial strength is vulnerable to adverse changes in underwriting and economic conditions.
Weak	C	C-	Assigned to insurance companies that have, in our opinion, a weak ability to meet their ongoing insurance obligations. Financial strength is very vulnerable to adverse changes in underwriting and economic conditions.
Poor	D	-	Assigned to insurance companies that have, in our opinion, a poor ability to meet their ongoing insurance obligations. Financial strength is extremely vulnerable to adverse changes in underwriting and economic conditions.

* Each Best's Financial Strength Rating Category from "A+" to "C" includes a Rating Notch to reflect a gradation of financial strength within the category. A Rating Notch is expressed with either a second plus "+" or a minus "-".

Financial Strength Non-Rating Designations

Designation Symbols	Designation Definitions
E	Status assigned to insurance companies that are publicly placed under a significant form of regulatory supervision, control or restraint - including cease and desist orders, conservatorship or rehabilitation, but not liquidation - that prevents conduct of normal ongoing insurance operations; an impaired insurer.
F	Status assigned to insurance companies that are publicly placed in liquidation by a court of law or by a forced liquidation; an impaired insurer.
S	Status assigned to rated insurance companies to suspend the outstanding FSR when sudden and significant events impact operations and rating implications cannot be evaluated due to a lack of timely or adequate information; or in cases where continued maintenance of the previously published rating opinion is in violation of evolving regulatory requirements.
NR	Status assigned to insurance companies that are not rated; may include previously rated insurance companies or insurance companies that have never been rated by A.M. Best.

Rating Disclosure – Use and Limitations

A Best's Credit Rating (BCR) is a forward-looking independent and objective opinion regarding an insurer's, issuer's or financial obligation's relative creditworthiness. The opinion represents a comprehensive analysis consisting of a quantitative and qualitative evaluation of balance sheet strength, operating performance, business profile and enterprise risk management or, where appropriate, the specific nature and details of a security. Because a BCR is a forward-looking opinion as of the date it is released, it cannot be considered as a fact or guarantee of future credit quality and therefore cannot be described as accurate or inaccurate. A BCR is a relative measure of risk that implies credit quality and is assigned using a scale with a defined population of categories and notches. Entities or obligations assigned the same BCR symbol developed using the same scale, should not be viewed as completely identical in terms of credit quality. Alternatively, they are alike in category (or notches within a category), but given there is a prescribed progression of categories (and notches) used in assigning the ratings of a much larger population of entities or obligations, the categories (notches) cannot mirror the precise subtleties of risk that are inherent within similarly rated entities or obligations. While a BCR reflects the opinion of A.M. Best Rating Services, Inc. (A.M. Best) of relative creditworthiness, it is not an indicator or predictor of defined impairment or default probability with respect to any specific insurer, issuer or financial obligation. A BCR is not investment advice, nor should it be construed as a consulting or advisory service, as such; it is not intended to be utilized as a recommendation to purchase, hold or terminate any insurance policy, contract, security or any other financial obligation, nor does it address the suitability of any particular policy or contract for a specific purpose or purchaser. Users of a BCR should not rely on it in making any investment decision; however, if used, the BCR must be considered as only one factor. Users must make their own evaluation of each investment decision. A BCR opinion is provided on an "as is" basis without any expressed or implied warranty. In addition, a BCR may be changed, suspended or withdrawn at any time for any reason at the sole discretion of A.M. Best.

BCRs are distributed via the A.M. Best website at www.ambest.com. For additional information regarding the development of a BCR and other rating-related information and definitions, including outlooks, modifiers, identifiers and affiliation codes, please refer to the report titled "Understanding Best's Credit Ratings" available at no charge on the A.M. Best website. BCRs are proprietary and may not be reproduced without permission.

of its operating performance and, ultimately, its exposure to capital volatility. Therefore, if a company is practicing sound risk management and executing its strategy effectively, it will preserve and build its balance sheet strength and perform successfully over the long term—both key elements of A.M. Best's ratings and the evaluation of risk management.

BEST'S ISSUER CREDIT RATING GUIDE – (ICR)

A Best's Issuer Credit Rating (ICR) is an independent opinion of an entity's ability to meet its ongoing financial obligations and can be issued on either a long- or short-term basis. A long-term ICR is an opinion of an entity's ability to meet its ongoing senior financial obligations, while a short-term ICR is an opinion of an entity's ability to meet its ongoing financial obligations with original maturities generally less than one year. An ICR is an opinion regarding the relative future credit risk of an entity. Credit risk is the risk that an entity may not meet its contractual financial obligations as they come due. An ICR does not address any other risk. In addition, an ICR is not a recommendation to buy, sell or hold any securities, contracts or any other financial obligations, nor does it address the suitability of any particular financial obligation for a specific purpose or purchaser. An ICR may be displayed with a rating identifier or modifier that denotes a unique aspect of the opinion.

Best's Long-Term Issuer Credit Rating (ICR) Scale

Rating Categories	Rating Symbols	Rating Notches*	Category Definitions
Exceptional	aaa	-	Assigned to entities that have, in our opinion, an exceptional ability to meet their ongoing senior financial obligations.
Superior	aa	aa+ / aa-	Assigned to entities that have, in our opinion, a superior ability to meet their ongoing senior financial obligations.
Excellent	a	a+ / a-	Assigned to entities that have, in our opinion, an excellent ability to meet their ongoing senior financial obligations.
Good	bbb	bbb+ / bbb-	Assigned to entities that have, in our opinion, a good ability to meet their ongoing senior financial obligations.
Fair	bb	bb+ / bb-	Assigned to entities that have, in our opinion, a fair ability to meet their ongoing senior financial obligations. Credit quality is vulnerable to adverse changes in industry and economic conditions.
Marginal	b	b+ / b-	Assigned to entities that have, in our opinion, a marginal ability to meet their ongoing senior financial obligations. Credit quality is vulnerable to adverse changes in industry and economic conditions.
Weak	ccc	ccc+ / ccc-	Assigned to entities that have, in our opinion, a weak ability to meet their ongoing senior financial obligations. Credit quality is vulnerable to adverse changes in industry and economic conditions.
Very Weak	cc	-	Assigned to entities that have, in our opinion, a very weak ability to meet their ongoing senior financial obligations. Credit quality is very vulnerable to adverse changes in industry and economic conditions.
Poor	c	-	Assigned to entities that have, in our opinion, a poor ability to meet their ongoing senior financial obligations. Credit quality is extremely vulnerable to adverse changes in industry and economic conditions.

Best's Long-Term Issuer Credit Rating Categories from "aa" to "ccc" include Rating Notches to reflect a gradation within the category to indicate whether credit quality is near the top or bottom of a particular Rating Category. Rating Notches are expressed with a "+" (plus) or "-" (minus).

Best's Short-Term Issuer Credit Rating (ICR) Scale

Rating Categories	Rating Symbols	Category Definitions
Strongest	AMB-1+	Assigned to entities that have, in our opinion, the strongest ability to repay their short-term financial obligations.
Outstanding	AMB-1	Assigned to entities that have, in our opinion, an outstanding ability to repay their short-term financial obligations.
Satisfactory	AMB-2	Assigned to entities that have, in our opinion, a satisfactory ability to repay their short-term financial obligations.
Adequate	AMB-3	Assigned to entities that have, in our opinion, an adequate ability to repay their short-term financial obligations; however, adverse industry or economic conditions likely will reduce their capacity to meet their financial commitments.
Questionable	AMB-4	Assigned to entities that have, in our opinion, questionable credit quality and are vulnerable to adverse economic or other external changes, which could have a marked impact on their ability to meet their financial commitments.

Long- and Short-Term Issuer Credit Non-Rating Designations

Designation Symbols	Designation Definitions
d	Status assigned to entities (excluding insurers) that are in default or when a bankruptcy petition or similar action has been filed and made public.
e	Status assigned to insurers that are publicly placed under a significant form of regulatory supervision, control or restraint - including cease and desist orders, conservatorship or rehabilitation, but not liquidation - that prevents conduct of normal ongoing operations; an impaired entity.
f	Status assigned to insurers that are publicly placed in liquidation by a court of law or by a forced liquidation; an impaired entity.
s	Status assigned to rated entities to suspend the outstanding ICR when sudden and significant events impact operations and rating implications cannot be evaluated due to a lack of timely or adequate information; or in cases where continued maintenance of the previously published rating opinion is in violation of evolving regulatory requirements.
nr	Status assigned to entities that are not rated; may include previously rated entities or entities that have never been rated by A.M. Best.

Rating Disclosure: Use and Limitations

A Best's Credit Rating (BCR) is a forward-looking independent and objective opinion regarding an insurer's, issuer's or financial obligation's relative creditworthiness. The opinion represents a comprehensive analysis consisting of a quantitative and qualitative evaluation of balance sheet strength, operating performance, business profile and enterprise risk management or, where appropriate, the specific nature and details of a security. Because a BCR is a forward-looking opinion as of the date it is released, it cannot be considered as a fact or guarantee of future credit quality and therefore cannot be described as accurate or inaccurate. A BCR is a relative measure of risk that implies credit quality and is assigned using a scale with a defined population of categories and notches. Entities or obligations assigned the same BCR symbol developed using the same scale, should not be viewed as completely identical in terms of credit quality. Alternatively, they are alike in category (or notches within a category), but given there is a prescribed progression of categories (and notches) used in assigning the ratings of a much larger population of entities or obligations, the categories (notches) cannot mirror the precise subtleties of the risk that are inherent within similarly rated entities or obligations. While a BCR reflects the opinion of A.M. Best Rating Services, Inc. (A.M. Best) of relative creditworthiness, it is not an indicator or predictor of defined impairment or default probability with respect to any specific insurer, issuer or financial obligation. A BCR is not investment advice, nor should it be construed as a consulting or advisory service, as such; it is not intended to be utilized as a recommendation to purchase, hold or terminate any insurance policy, contract, security or any other financial obligation, nor does it address the suitability of any particular policy or contract for a specific purpose or purchaser. Users of a BCR should not rely on it in making any investment decision; however, if used, the BCR must be considered as only one factor. Users must make their own evaluation of each investment decision. A BCR opinion is provided on an "as is" basis without any expressed or implied warranty. In addition, a BCR may be changed, suspended or withdrawn at any time for any reason at the sole discretion of A.M. Best.

BCRs are distributed via the A.M. Best website at *www.ambest.com*. For additional information regarding the development of a BCR and other rating-related information and definitions, including outlooks, modifiers, identifiers and affiliation codes, please refer to the report titled "Understanding Best's Credit Ratings" available at no charge on the A.M. Best website. BCRs are proprietary and may not be reproduced without permission.

Copyright © 2017 by A.M. Best Company, Inc. and/or its affiliates. ALL RIGHTS RESERVED.   Version 101317

A.M. Best's Insurance Information Products and Services

Insight and Advantage

A.M. Best provides dozens of insurance information resources that help everyone from C-level executives to independent agents work more effectively and productively. The resources provide unique insight—based on more than a century of exclusive focus on the insurance industry—that delivers a competitive advantage to those who need to know the why as well as the what, for tomorrow as well as today.

Below is a sampling of some of A.M. Best's most widely used and highly regarded products and services. For more product offerings, visit *www.ambest.com/sales.*

Best's Insurance Reports®: A.M. Best's flagship product provides in-depth ***Best's Credit Reports*** on thousands of insurers, reinsurers and groups around the world. The reports present a company's current Best's Credit Rating, a Rating Rationale that explains why the rating was assigned, commentary on the company's risk management strategy, an analysis of its balance sheet strength, and more. *Best's Insurance Reports* is available online via *BestLink*®, A.M. Best's sophisticated data delivery and integration platform.

- ***A.M. Best's Financial Suite****:* This family of databases presents detailed information from the financial statements of thousands of insurance entities. *Financial Suite* products are all accessible online via *BestLink*. Custom presentations of data are also available.
- ***Best's Statement File – US****:* presents complete statement data for U.S. insurers; additional databases focus on market share, loss reserves, expenses and investments.

Financial information on more than 16,000 non-U.S. insurers worldwide is presented in *Best's Statement File – Global.*

Best's Statement File – Canada: offers regulatory data from filings made with the Office of the Superintendent of Financial Institutions (OSFI) for hundreds of Canadian property/casualty or life/health insurers.

Other region-specific editions of *Best's Statement File* cover the United Kingdom and Latin America, as well as Asia-Pacific and the Middle East/North Africa regions.

Best's Capital Adequacy Ratio Model – Property/Casualty, US: This desktop application provides insight into how changing conditions can affect a company's future claims-paying ability with the same base model A.M. Best analysts use to calculate the Best's Capital Adequacy Ratio (BCAR) score for single and group U.S. property/casualty companies. A.M. Best also offers *Best's Capital Adequacy Ratio Model –Universal* for the non-U.S. life and nonlife sectors.

***Best's Aggregates & Averages – US & Canada (Property/Casualty* and *Life/Health* editions):** This vital benchmarking and strategic-planning tool presents current and historical consolidated data for the property/casualty or life/health industry.

***Best's Key Rating Guide – US & Canada (Property/Casualty* and *Life/Health* editions):** This classic resource offers, online and in print, five years of key financial figures and Best's Credit Ratings for thousands of insurance companies and HMOs—plus personalized reports that display information on individual companies in a format ideal for client presentations and proposals.

***Best's Underwriting Guide* and *Best's Loss Control Manual:** These online risk management resources provide detailed reports on hundreds of businesses, industries and municipal services, written from either the underwriter's or loss control engineer's point of view.

***Best's Insurance News & Analysis:** This subscription-based service provides the full scope of A.M. Best's award-winning news and industry research, all accessible through a streamlined web portal. The following are some products the service includes:

- *Best's Journal,* a compilation of ratings-related research and analysis.
- *BestWeek*®, a recap of the top stories for the global insurance industry in three focused editions (*Global, Regulatory* and *Asia-Pacific*).
- *Best's Special Reports* and *Best's Statistical Studies*, in-depth coverage of critical topics from an analytical or data-driven approach.
- *Best's Review*®, A.M. Best's award-winning monthly insurance magazine.
- *BestDay*®, a digest of insurance news from the past 24 hours.

A.M. Best also publishes a variety of online reports on individual companies, by state/by line market segments, peer group composites and other selections of information to meet your research and analysis needs. Visit www.ambest.com/sales for a complete overview of all that A.M. Best has to offer, or call (800) 424-2378 or (908) 439-2200, ext. 5742.

The Six Habits of Risk Deniers

The warnings came by the hundreds. Evacuate or face the potential consequences of the large, destructive and deadly hurricane barreling up the East Coast in October 2012. But many chose the latter, ignoring evacuation orders issued days before Hurricane Sandy became one of the costliest hurricanes in U.S. history. Even New Jersey Governor Chris Christie called the decisions of those remaining in harm's way "both stupid and selfish."

But actions like that are more common than you'd think, said Howard Kunreuther and Robert Meyer, co-authors of the book, "*The Ostrich Paradox*."

Instinctively, humans tend to think bad things will happen to others—not themselves, said Meyer, who is a Frederick H. Ecker/Metlife Insurance professor of marketing at the Wharton School of the University of Pennsylvania.

Our ability to foresee and protect against Mother Nature's forces has never been greater. Yet while scientific and analytical abilities to forecast natural catastrophes have grown, human life and monetary losses from those calamities have increased in recent years.

Individuals located in hazard-prone areas consistently fail to heed the warnings and do not protect themselves and their communities against the devastating consequences from natural catastrophes, said Kunreuther, James G. Dinan professor of decision sciences and public policy at Wharton.

Beyond physical preparations, such as stockpiling flashlights, batteries and water, individuals in disaster-prone areas need to be mentally prepared, said the book's authors, who are also co-directors of the Wharton Risk Management and Decision Processes Center. "We need to understand the psychological limitations that prevent us from being better prepared for disasters. Once we do, we can develop ways to better adapt to those restraints."

How did you come up with the title of the book; and does it mean that we shouldn't be sticking our heads in the sand when it comes to disasters?

Meyer: For many years, the metaphor we used during our presentations on disaster preparedness and the reasons why people don't ready themselves for those events was that individuals behave like ostriches by putting their heads in the sand. But it actually turns out that's giving ostriches a bad rap. They don't stick their heads in

Howard Kunreuther

BEST

the sand; rather, they're extremely good at dealing with risk. As humongous, flightless birds, you'd think that ostriches would be sitting ducks out in the plains of Africa. But they've been able to adapt to that limitation with their extremely fast ground speed and risk-avoidance strategies like lying completely flat to hide from predators.

Humans need to find ways to acknowledge and overcome our cognitive and psychological limitations that prevent us from preparing for disasters. If we can do that, then we can behave like ostriches.

Why are humans so poor at dealing with disastrous risks and what can we do to change that?

Kunreuther: The systematic biases and simple decision rules that we use in dealing with the world work well when focusing on many of our recurring daily decisions, but we do poorly when preparing for low-probability, high-consequence events, such as severe natural disasters where we have had limited, if any, personal experience. The first part of the book examines behavioral biases that deter us from appropriate disaster planning. By recognizing those biases, we can design ways to overcome them and better handle catastrophes.

What are the six biases that lead individuals, communities and institutions to make grave errors that can cost lives?

Meyer: The first is myopia, or the difficulty understanding the long-term consequences of events. Next is amnesia—the tendency to quickly forget things that happened in the past; inertia is where we maintain what we're now doing—so if we haven't protected ourselves in the past we'll continue with the status quo until something happens; simplification is not looking at all of the information when making decisions; and herding is where we look to others for guidance on decision-making. Finally, optimism is the idea that people often underestimate risk probabilities. It's probably the most damaging bias because the more we ignore worst-case scenarios and think bad things will only happen to others, the less able we are to prepare.

In the book you talk about how we fail to evacuate when advised, fail to build safely in hazard-prone areas, fail to purchase insurance and fail to wear helmets, and that we would rather avoid the risk of crying wolf than sound an alarm. Despite the fact that our ability to foresee and protect against natural catastrophes has never been greater, we continue to ignore the warnings, with devastating consequences. Can you explain that contradiction?

Meyer: The science of meteorology has progressed since the turn of the last century; organizations like the National Oceanic and Atmospheric Administration now have great accuracy in forecasting the path of a storm.

But at the same time, financial and human losses caused by disasters continue to rise. Despite scientific advances, there hasn't been a parallel increase in human response to warnings that come from NOAA and other organizations. Often warnings come out that we don't fully understand. We're focusing a lot on the science of the hazards and not as much on the psychology of how people prepare for them.

By Lori Chordas

Made in the USA
Monee, IL
19 September 2019